Quilts

California Bound, California Made 1840–1940

Quilts

California Bound, California Made 1840–1940

SANDI FOX

FIDM Museum & Library, Inc.

LOS ANGELES

Published in conjunction with the exhibition
*Quilts: California Bound, California Made
1840–1940*, organized by Sandi Fox and The Fashion Institute of Design & Merchandising/FIDM,
Los Angeles, and presented at the institute's
Museum & Galleries October 1–December 6,
2002.

This publication and the exhibition were funded
with a generous gift from Helen and Peter Bing.

ISBN: 0-9719184-0-6
Library of Congress Control Number: 2002107228

TITLE PAGE: *The Machado Quilt* (page 80)
PAGE 14: *The Bidwell Mansion's Quilt* (page 112)
PAGE 26: *The "Stars and Swags" Quilt* (page 30)
PAGE 58: *Sarah Ann Beegle's Quilt* (page 72)
PAGE 86: *The Hayes Family Quilts, "Crossed Sashing"*
(page 94)
PAGE 116: *The Cigar Ribbons Quilt* (page 142)
PAGE 148: *The Sacramento Valley Sugan* (page 160)
PAGE 168: *The Mount Wilson Observatory Quilt*
(page 188)

FIDM Museum & Library, Inc.
919 South Grand Avenue
Los Angeles, California 90015
http://fashionmuseum.FIDM.org

LIMITED EDITION

Contents

*This quilt appears in the book only.

The Chinoiserie Quilt, probably the
United States, early nineteenth century,
cotton; pieced, appliquéd, and quilted,
104 x 99½ in. (264.2 x 252.7 cm)
*Collection of the Natural History Museum
of Los Angeles County*

Preface

FROM THE BEGINNING, California was a gathering place for quilts and bedcovers from throughout the United States, brought first in covered wagons and great sailing vessels, and on the backs of mules across the Isthmus of Panama. And once women arrived in the West, they began—almost at once—to re-establish their most cherished domestic traditions; quiltmaking was high among them. Quilts that had been bound for California were unpacked and soon were joined by quilts made in those new and often challenging surroundings. California's pioneers all came from somewhere else, and so did the quilts they brought with them. Those, and the quilts they made when they arrived, became, simply, California's quilts. It is that richly diverse quilted legacy, established between 1840 and 1940, that provided the impetus for this foray into California's past.

THE CHINOISERIE QUILT

As with so many of California's quilts, the *Chinoiserie Quilt* came to California in incremental journeys. Several factors, such as its large size, point to the quilt's early date: the central-medallion style is appropriate to the earliest of nineteenth-century quilts (it suggests a strong English influence, if not actually an English origin); significantly, it is pieced and finely quilted with a two-ply linen thread (now grossly degraded); and it is constructed of very early English block-printed cottons. Although the fabric is now in a seriously deteriorated state, the motifs clearly exhibit certain identifying characteristics of an early date. Cut-chintz floral motifs are in abundance, both in sprigs and sprays (FIG. 1), and throughout, the color green is formed by blue, "pencilled" (painted) over yellow. Wonderful, feathered birds have been cut from other floral chintz and appliquéd to a white ground; distinctive with their bright, dark-centered, round eyes, they are perched throughout the quilt on short, arborescent branches (FIG. 2).

FIGURE 1
The Chinoiserie Quilt (detail)

Most distinctive of all are the appliquéd figurative and architectural elements of *chinoiserie*. In the seventeenth century, soon after the establishment of the Dutch and East Indian trading companies, the decorative arts craze for all things from the Orient became pervasive. The images on the porcelain and the lacquerware appeared also on silks and cotton furnishing fabrics, rococo elements with figures in fanciful, leisurely settings (FIG. 3). Here they are all contained within a stripe of early (possibly 1807–10) honey-combed leaves that form the outermost of the numerous inner borders (FIG. 4).

Another *chinoiserie* textile, of later origin, appeared on a friendship block (FIG. 5), inscribed "Mrs Jane L / Ayers. / 1848 / Omit no opportunity, / for good / M. [?] B." It is one of a small, unassembled group said to have come from the California gold fields near Placerville.[1]

FIGURE 4
The Chinoiserie Quilt (detail)

That the *Chinoiserie Quilt* has survived for two centuries is in itself a wonder, as are the circumstances of its survival: that it was chosen, more than once, to be packed for a journey westward; that it was selected— like other quilts catalogued in this book— from all those other treasures that had to be left behind; that each subsequent generation carried it west until it came, at last, to California; and that, once here, it hung for decades nailed to a wall. Surely it is a quiet reverence for the relics of our quilted past that has saved this quilt. It is that quilted past, California bound and California made, that both this exhibition and these pages celebrate.

SANDI FOX
Los Angeles

FIGURE 5
Friendship Blocks, provenance unknown; top block marked 1848, signed by Mrs. Jane L. Ayers, cotton, appliquéd, inked inscriptions, 10 x 10 in. (25.4 x 25.4 cm)

NOTE

1.   Thomas Frye, ed., *American Quilts: A Handmade Legacy*, exhibition catalogue (Oakland: Oakland Museum of California, 1981).

Lenders to the Exhibition

Autry Museum of Western Heritage

Mildred Breitbarth and Linda Breitbarth

California State Parks, Bidwell Mansion State Historic Park

California State Parks, Sutter's Fort

The Harkness Family

Los Angeles County Museum of Art

Marshall Gold Discovery State Historic Park

Member, American Decorative Arts Forum of Northern California

Cressie Ellen Mendes

Natural History Museum of Los Angeles County

Oakland Museum of California

Private Collection

Mike Reinoso

Riverside Municipal Museum

San Diego Historical Society

Herb Wallerstein

The Waters Family

Acknowledgments

THIS BOOK IS DEDICATED to the memory of Maggie Pexton Murray, the late director of the FIDM Museum & Galleries. I am very grateful to the Board of Administration of The Fashion Institute of Design & Merchandising/FIDM for facilitating an exhibition that was Maggie's vision as well as my own.

It has been a great pleasure to work with the Museum's new director, Robert Nelson. His staff has been endlessly helpful, most particularly Jill Quinn, Kevin Jones, Tara Callow, Horacio Avila, and Michael Black.

The quilts have been drawn from distinguished collections, both public and private, throughout California. Colleagues from the lending institutions have been exceptionally generous in facilitating the loans to the exhibition: Linda Strauss and Laurie German, the Autry Museum of Western Heritage; Shirley Kendall and Judy Crain, the Bidwell Mansion State Historic Park; Nancy Thomas and the staff of the Conservation Department and the Department of Costumes and Textiles, the Los Angeles County Museum of Art; Ken Simmons, the Marshall Gold Discovery State Historic Park; Dr. Janet Fireman and Beth Werling, the Natural History Museum of Los Angeles County; Inez Brooks-Meyers, Diane Curry, and Bill McMorris, the Oakland Museum of California; Dr. H. Vincent Moses, Dr. Brenda Focht, and Lynn Voorheis, the Riverside Municipal Museum; Tammie Bennett, the San Diego Historical Society; and Mike Tucker and Melani Wilkie, Sutter's Fort. I am deeply grateful to them all. I am grateful as well to the private lenders; the exhibition is honored by their participation.

Research for this publication was conducted throughout California and the western states, as was the selection of comparative material and images. I was supported in that undertaking by a great many colleagues and curators, research librarians and registrars, whose advice and assistance, both within their fields of specialty and without, have been absolutely invaluable to this project: Steve Baker, the Monrovia Historical Society; Peter Blodgett and Brooke Black, the Huntington Library in San Marino; Timothy Burgard and Sue Grinols, the Fine Arts Museums of San Francisco; John Cahoon, the Seaver Center for Western History Research at the Natural History Museum of Los Angeles County; Dennis Copeland, archivist, the Monterey Public Library; Melva Felchlin, the Research Center at the Autry Museum of Western Heritage in Los Angeles; John Gonzales and the exceptional staff at the California State Library in Sacramento; Karen Mehring, the Folsom History Museum; Kris Quist, the Monterey State Historic Park; Hema Ramachandran, Sherman-Fairchild Library, the California Institute of Technology; Militia Rios-Samaniego, the Discovery Museum History Center in Sacramento; Matt Severson, the Academy of Motion Picture Arts and Sciences Library in Los Angeles; Dennis Smith and the Archives staff at the Church of Jesus Christ of

Latter-Day Saints in Salt Lake City; the staff at the Bancroft Library, the University of California, Berkeley; and Jack Enyart, Catherine Kypta and Lenore Dean, Caroline Lieberman, Pat Shuman, Michael Simmons, Camilla Smith, Laurel Tanner, Carol Verbeck, Emily Vigas, and Carol Williams.

Three of the most significant of the selected quilts presented considerable damage and/or deterioration; I determined they could not safely or aesthetically be exhibited without extensive conservation. Through a very generous grant, the Southern California Council of Quilt Guilds underwrote the necessary work; additional funding was provided by the Textile Group of Los Angeles. Conservator Sharon Shore applied her consummate skills to the *Chinoiserie Quilt*, the *"Stars and Swags" Quilt*, and the *Cowboys Quilt*, with results far beyond even my most optimistic expectations.

My husband, John Fox, served as research photographer and fellow traveler; a partner in my life and in my work, he read with me in libraries and research rooms up and down the state of California.

The exhibition's stunning installation was designed by Bernard Kester. The quiltmakers would have been so pleased!

Each page of this book shines with the exceptional sensitivities of its designer, Sandy Bell, and the splendid photographs of Steve Oliver; we have worked on projects together for over a decade. To this familiar circle was added a brilliant editor, Shelly Kale; every aspect of the text has been enriched by her perceptive comments and suggestions.

The exhibition and this publication were made possible by a gift from Helen and Peter Bing. This is the third major exhibition of American quilts they have underwritten; collectors, connoisseurs, and scholars are in their debt, as am I.

Notes to the Reader

Great care has been given to the task of transcribing the inscriptions found on the quilts and the bedcovers. The same is true of the material quoted from handwritten and early printed sources. In each instance, grammar, punctuation, and spelling are presented as they appear.

Throughout, quilt measurements are given in both inches and centimeters; length precedes width.

Several of the quilts, such as the *Boardman Quilt*, have appeared in other works by the author in which the text touched—often extensively—on other aspects of the quilt than those addressed here. Additional photographs often appear as well. Footnotes alert the reader to this additional material.

PART 1

Beginnings

$\mathcal{Q}$UILTS CAME EARLY TO CALIFORNIA, and they came by diverse routes. They came by wagon, of course, and on ships around the horn, and on mules across the Isthmus of Panama, and decades later, when the tracks of the transcontinental railroad stretched to the Pacific, they came by train as well. And it is quite probable that the earliest of all came by the simplest of means, in a bedroll on the back of an adventurer's horse.

As quilts came by diverse means, so did the fabrics from which early California quilt-makers would make their new quilts. If quiltmaking in the homes these pioneering women had left behind was a matter of pleasure, in this new land it would become a challenge as well. The equipment they required—needles and pins, thread, and a small scissors—could be carried in their pockets, but fabric had to be got. Pieces of cloth could be found in the trunks they had packed, traded with a new neighbor, bought off the sparse shelves of a small general store, or—most surprisingly—pulled from the sea.

"Callicoes of Every Colour"

BAY OF MONTEREY UPPER CALIFORNIA

FIGURE I
William Smyth (1800–1877), *Bay of Monterey, Upper California*, 1827, watercolor, 8¾ x 14 in. (22.2 x 35.6 cm) *Courtesy of the Bancroft Library, University of California, Berkeley*

IT WAS THE STORIES OF THE LAND, and of the commercial fortunes to be made, that brought Americans to California long before 1848, when gold was discovered at Sutter's Mill. By 1822, a half-century of Spanish authority had ended in Alta California (Upper California) and Mexico had declared Monterey an open port. The resulting increase in trade brought an influx of eastern and foreign vessels to the bay and to the city's customhouse.

In this pastoral view of Monterey during the Mexican era, 1822–46 (FIG. 1), we can see in the distance a Russian brig, a Yankee schooner, and the *H.M.S. Blossom*. The primary trade was in hides and tallow, but on July 27, 1845, it was a cargo of cloth that would preoccupy Monterey's merchants.

> Monterey August 26 1845
> [Thomas Larkin to] Mr. J. J. Jarvis
> *Sir*
> The English Schr "Star of the West" Capt. Wm Atherton of Weymouth seven months from Liverpool, struck on the rocks at Point Lobos, (10 miles South of this port) about 10 oclock at night the 27 of last month. The men left in the Boat without being able to save only the cloths they had on. The Captain presented himself to my house about 1 oclock next afternoon. By 4 oclock I had three Boats with people along side the wreck. I found all her rigging whole & sail set, washing against the rocks which were very high. The whole deck was under water, the

railing of the vessel and chains coverd with Callicoes of every colour which was
coming out of the wreck as the Boxes broke up.[1]

Thomas Oliver Larkin, a significant figure in California's history as the
state's governance moved from Mexican to American, was the most prominent
merchant in Monterey and, at this time, the U.S. consul to Mexico there. He
built his home (FIG. 2) facing the *calle principal*, the road on which the oxcarts
took the hides from the nearby ranchos down to the beach. It was the first
two-story building in Monterey and one of the first in California. Begun in
December 1834, the first floor served as a retail store and a central staircase led
upstairs to the family's residence. Larkin's wife, Rachel, was very pleased to
have a home in the New England style of her youth.[2] The view in an 1842 lithograph (FIG. 3) was originally drawn for Larkin, and his building (with the
adjacent private garden) is, not surprisingly, featured most prominently, near
the lower left-hand margin.

Larkin left extensive commercial correspondence concerning the wreck of
the *Star of the West*, and in so doing established a record of the dramatic introduction of a substantial amount of fine English "Callicoes of every colour" into
Monterey in 1845.

The *Star of the West* was, in fact, bound for Mazatlán, Mexico, where the
duties on the reported $120,000 cargo would have been excessively high.
Authorities in the customhouse in Monterey had in all probability agreed to
allow a reduced valuation in their port to the benefit of both the authorities
there and John Parrott, the U.S. consul in Mazatlán, to whom the cargo had
been consigned.[3] The fabric had been destined to be carried on mules to Mexico's interior and the dry goods, therefore, had been packed in medium-sized,
waterproof bundles; although the bulk of the cargo was lost, the large shipment
of cotton cloth emerged in extraordinarily good condition.

FIGURE 2
Thomas Larkin's home and store in
Monterey, California, undated
photograph *Courtesy of the Monterey State
Historic Park Collection*

HARBOUR and CITY of MONTEREY, California 1842.

In 1845, John A. Swan, a British sailor who had come to Monterey two years earlier, wrote a contemporaneous account of the salvage operations of the precious textiles:

> a great deal of the dry goods were saved from the wreck not much the worse, but the bulk of the cargo was lost. Mr. T O Larkin then U S Consul took charge of the wrecking business. there was no quaarreling or fighting, ever[y]thing was carried to Mr Larkins store in Monterey, and the dry goods were washed in fresh water . . . dry goods at that time fetched a high price in California and the dry goods of the Star of the West were of very good quality. some of the people engaged in wrecking sold their shares in the goods saved to store keepers in Monterey as well as in other parts of the country before they were divided. some opened dry goods stores with the goods saved from the star of the west . . . some people who have become wealthy since in California were engaged [in] fishing for dry goods from the Schooner Star of the west.[4]

Larkin began at once to capitalize on his salvage efforts. On July 31 (four days after the event) he wrote to James Watson, another Monterey merchant:

> I am trying to save from the Sea, the property belonging to the late English Schooner "Star of the West" wrecked on the Rocks of point Lobos during the night of the twenty seventh instant, about ten miles from this port.
>
> These goods are brought up by grappling, and towed on shore. They come ashore in Boxes, Bales and peices one foot long and upwards in lenght. The people who are wrecking claim one third. There maybe five to ten thousands peices saved, according to the weather for twenty days to come.

You will pleased inform me what price in cash paid on delivery of the goods you will give for the following named goods taking them at high water mark where the wreckers land them and in the state they are landed. I am Sir Your Most Obedient Servant[5]

The following day, Mr. Watson replied. He indicated, for example, a willingness to pay $2.13 each for one dozen pieces of "Figured Muslin" and $2.00 each for a dozen pieces of "Calico prints." A similar letter to W. D. M. Howard on the American ship *California* brought a slightly higher offer ($2.50) for the "Figured Muslin" (the fabric eventually sold for a much greater sum) and his response informs us that the muslin was 32 inches wide, the calico 36.[6] To our great regret, no specific designs were described, but even John Swan, the sailor, had recognized that the calico was of a "very good quality."

A Swiss immigrant, Captain John A. Sutter (FIG. 4) had reached Monterey in 1839 and advised General Juan Bautista Alvarado, the Mexican governor of Monterey (1836–42), of his wish to establish a colony in Alta California on the Sacramento River. Since Sutter's intention coincided with the general's wish that the area be subdued and settled, he readily agreed to the request. Sutter returned to Monterey in June 1841; in return for his success and services he was granted Mexican citizenship and title to the 11 square leagues of land (about 50,000 acres) on which he had located. Sutter thereafter purchased the Russian possessions in California known as Ross and Bodega, acquiring a "vast extent of real estate, 2000 cattle, 1000 horses, fifty mules and 2500 sheep."[7] All were added to his already substantial holdings in his "New Helvetia." Intending to fortify himself, Sutter constructed a fort. Completed in 1844, Sutter's Fort became a place of rendezvous for overland travelers; it acquired a military significance as well.

Sutter, although perpetually in overwhelming debt, was a commercial presence in the area, always privy to the events in Monterey; on October 7 he wrote to an associate, "Whole Monterey is full of Goods from the wrecked Vessel."[8] A few days before the *Star of the West* went down, he had written to Thomas Larkin with a "List of Articles wanted at New Helvetia." He listed over seventy different articles in various quantities, from the irons for a sawmill to one thousand fishhooks, and he included "20 pieces of dark colored good Callico."[9] Late in September he wrote to Larkin, "Some of the Damaged Goods of the wreked Vessel would answer very well for Indians if it is cheaper."[10] The market in the salvaged fabric continued for months, and surely Sutter would have sought to secure some of the finest of the "Callicoes of every colour" for the store at his fort. Immigrants continued to settle around New Helvetia; as Sutter somewhat casually documented four months later, east on the American River there were American quiltmakers.

FIGURE 4
Captain John A. Sutter (1803–1880), from a photograph by Bradley & Rulofson, *The Century Magazine* 66, no. 2 (December 1890): 163

NOTES

1. George P. Hammond, ed., *The Larkin Papers: Personal, Business and Official Correspondence of Thomas Oliver Larkin, Merchant and United States Consul in California*, vol. 3 (Berkeley and Los Angeles: University of California Press, 1952), pp. 324–25.

2. The building, and the distinctive Monterey Style of adobe architecture it established, is detailed and further illustrated in Harlan Hague and David J. Langum, *Thomas O. Larkin: A Life of Patriotism and Profit in Old California* (Norman and London: University of Oklahoma Press, 1990), pp. 46–49.

3. William Heath Davis, *Seventy-Five Years in California* (San Francisco: John Howell, 1929), p. 163.

4. John A. Swan, "Wreck of the Star of the West," MS quoted in Robert J. Parker, "The Wreck of the Star of the West," *The Quarterly: Historical Society of Southern California* 23, no. 1 (March 1941): 26.

5. Hammond, *The Larkin Papers*, p. 288.

6. Ibid., p. 289. The other fabrics offered were pieces of mixed cotton cloth, book muslin, velvet, English silk, vesting, and "White Imperial." Florence M. Montgomery, in *Textiles in America: 1650–1870* (New York: W. W. Norton, 1984), p. 262, identifies Imperial satin (closely woven cotton fabric), Imperial serge (lightweight twill of worsted and wool), Imperial shirting (bleached cotton shirting), and Imperial tape (stout cotton tape).

7. Hon. Wm. J. Davis, *Illustrated History of Sacramento County, California* (Chicago: Lewis Publishing Company, 1890), p. 9.

8. J. A. Sutter to P. B. Reading, New Helvetia, California, October 7, 1845, MS in California State Library, Sacramento, Calif.

9. Hammond, *The Larkin Papers*, p. 284.

10. Ibid, p. 365.

"All the People Attended the Quilting at Mrs. Montgomery's"

IRONICALLY, IT WAS TWO MEN that provided the earliest known documentation of a quilting party in California. One mention appears in a business journal, *New Helvetia Diary: A Record of Events Kept By John A. Sutter And His Clerks at New Helvetia, California, From September 9, 1845 to May 25, 1848*, in the entry for Thursday, January 29, 1846:

> All the people attended the quilting at Mrs. Montgomery's—Mr. Loker went up and delivered 100 Sheep to Capt. Leidsdorff—and Mr. Rheusau from Feather River.[1]

The second appears in a letter, written in New Helvetia that same day by Captain Sutter to his friend, P. B. Reading (then encamped on the San Joaquin River):

> To day was a quilting at Montgomeris, the whole Neighborhood was invited, and a great many was there present, I keept house and let go nearly all the Gentlemen.[2]

Although it is frequently referred to as such, we cannot confirm this to be the *first* "quilting" in California. Such gatherings, held for purpose and pleasure, were an important part of the life left behind[3]; it is probable that smaller, informal events already had been enjoyed by the few first pioneers. The historical significance of Mrs. Montgomery's quilting party lies primarily in its memorializing—the recording of an early transplantation of a social tradition, chosen for inclusion in both business records and personal correspondence.

By noting that the whole "Neighborhood" was invited, Captain Sutter observed an early sense of community, even in the far-flung reaches of his New Helvetia (FIG. 1). Some families lived in and around the fort while others established themselves along the rivers and elsewhere. Allen Montgomery worked for Sutter, who sent him into the pine woods on the south fork of the American River, probably near what is now Coloma, California, to lumber and produce shingles for the fort.[4]

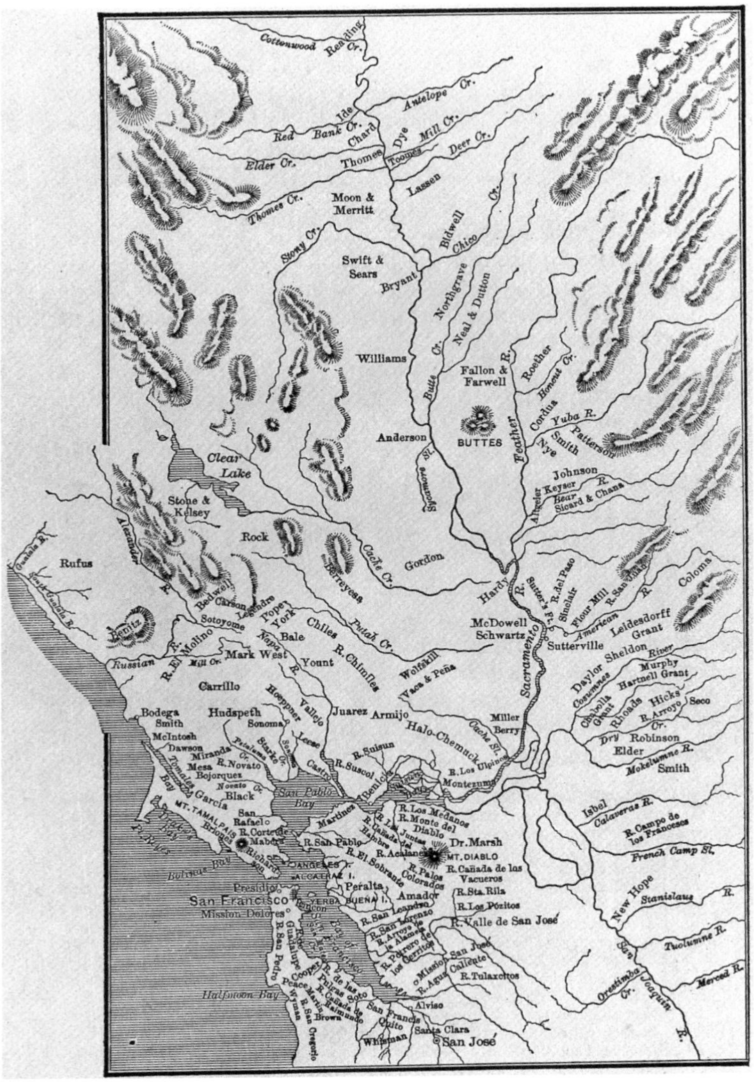

FIGURE I
Cartographer unknown, *Central California in 1848*, 6½ x 4¾ in. (16.5 x 12.1 cm) Collection of the Bancroft Library, University of California, Berkeley

It was there the Montgomerys built a cabin and where Sarah Montgomery eventually held her "quilting." These were traditionally festive events for both men and women with food and music and dancing; surely "the Gentlemen" and their wives would have ridden almost any distance to attend. A variety of historical sources[5] identify at least twenty-two women probably living within a day's journey and likely to have vied for a spot at the quilting frame—they were, in all likelihood, among California's first quiltmakers:

Jane Elkins Bonney (Mrs. Jarvis)	Sarah Armstrong Montgomery (Mrs. Allen)
Esther Townsend Bonney (Mrs. Truman)	Mary Bolger Murphy (Mrs. John)
Miss Bonney (later Mrs. Allen Sanders)	Ann Martin Murphy (Mrs. James)
Frances Kelsey Buzzell (Mrs. Joseph)	Margaret Nash (Mrs. John?)
Nancy Ann Hess Chamberlain (Mrs. John)	Mrs. R. K. Payne
Lizzie Sumner Davis (Mrs. George)	Mrs. Felix Scott
Eliza Marshall Gregson (Mrs. James)	Mrs. Mary Sinclair (Mrs. John)
Mrs. Daniel Leahy	Mrs. Eugene Skinner
Mrs. Perry McCoon	Mrs. Ann Marshall Smith
Margaret Pyles McDowell (Mrs. James)	Mrs. William Isaac Tustin
Mary Ann Marshall	America Kelsey Wyman (Mrs. George)

FIGURE 2
James and Eliza Gregson, Petaluma, California, ca. 1860, photograph, size unavailable *Courtesy of California State Parks, Sutter's Fort*

They were pioneers—mothers and daughters, sisters and sisters-in-law, wives and widows. Some were educated, others were illiterate. Some were married to alcoholics, others to men of great ambition who would develop their own, and California's, wealth. They had packed little of a personal nature, but they possessed a set of abilities—brought or acquired—that assured their survival. Important among these, when there were families to be clothed, was the ability to sew, plain and fancy.

We can only guess what the ladies wore to Mrs. Montgomery's quilting party. The January 5 entry of *New Helvetia Diary* recorded that "Mrs. Montgomery came to the fort"[6] probably delivering invitations, so they had time to decide but little opportunity for much choice. One of the likely participants, Eliza Gregson (FIG. 2), had felt the uncomfortable pinch of poverty for almost all of her married life: "We turned our thoughts westword. . . .We started leaveing all behind with just 18 dollers in 10 cents peices." Her dress would have no doubt been of the very plain sort—"our clothes we had to patch untill the original peice could scarcely be found"[7]; others had found room in their trunk for at least one good dress.

Cotton dresses of this period are exceedingly rare. This charming, late 1840s example (FIG. 3), from the collection at Sutter's Fort, exemplifies the finest of the dressmaker's skills: beautifully hand-sewn, the piped neckline, waistline, and

dropped shoulder line are in the style of the period; cartridge pleating is used
extensively throughout, on the sleeves as they fit into the armscye and at the
skirt's waistline (folded over for additional fullness at the hipline) where it is
attached to the bodice; gathered inner cap sleeves are finished with a decorative
scallop, edged with a buttonhole stitch—an elegant touch observable only to
the wearer![8] Several of the techniques used on this exquisite garment—such as
the fine hand-worked seams and the elegant piping (FIG. 4)—would be applied
as well to California's quilts.

Although no quilt is known to exist that can be traced to the day's
endeavors "at Mrs. Montgomery's," if one did, it would look no different than
what had been made in Arkansas and Missouri and Illinois—this was the
nature of quiltmaking as it came to, and flourished in, California.

Of those remarkable pioneer women who lived in and around Sutter's Fort in 1846, the most remarkable of all was the hostess of the "quilting," Sarah Armstrong Montgomery.[9] She was born on a farm in southern Ohio in August 1825. When she was nine years old, her Methodist parents, who were born in New York, moved the family to western Indiana. Five years later (even then it seemed to be the nature of many Americans to be always on the move), they crossed the Mississippi River to farm in western Missouri on the edge of Indian Territory. When her father died in 1842, at sixteen, Sarah became a hired girl in the home of a St. Joseph physician, Dr. John B. Townsend. In 1843, she married a gunsmith, Allen Montgomery, ten years her senior, and in August 1844, they set out with the Townsend family to travel west with the Stevens Party. Sarah was nineteen years old, and she was California bound!

The incredible, well-documented journey of the Stevens Party brought the Montgomerys to Sutter's Fort; aside from the "quilting" and three visits to Sutter's Fort mentioned in the *New Helvetia Diary*, we know almost nothing of Sarah's life there. But while their husbands were off participating in the Bear Flag Rebellion,[10] Sarah and Eliza Gregson briefly moved in with Mrs. Daniel Leahy; those days were recalled later by Eliza in her "memories." It is from her pages that we learn Sarah could not write:

FIGURE 4
Sutter's Fort dress (detail)

> [Mrs. Leahy] asked me if I would teach her little girls to write as she did not know how herselfe. I told her Yes I would & was very glad for I had no employment so at it I went during that time Mrs. Montgomery would watch us with great interest. one day she says to me will you teach me Mrs. Gregson. I looked at her to see if she was in enerst & I told her yes if you want to learn. She said if you will teach me how to write I will do something very big for you if I am able. So I fulfilled my part but she forgot her part.[11]

Allen Montgomery set sail for Honolulu in 1847 on board the *Julia*; no further record is found of him.[12] Perhaps he simply abandoned Sarah, who thereafter referred to herself as a widow. But Sarah evidently was a strongwilled and purposeful woman (as a member of the Stevens Party, she had, after all, pushed herself over the snowy summit of the Sierra Nevadas), and in October 1849, she married a San Francisco millionaire, Talbot Green, with whom she had one son. Unfortunately, two years later Green was revealed to be a perfect scoundrel—an embezzler and a bigamist with another family, and another name, in Pennsylvania.[13]

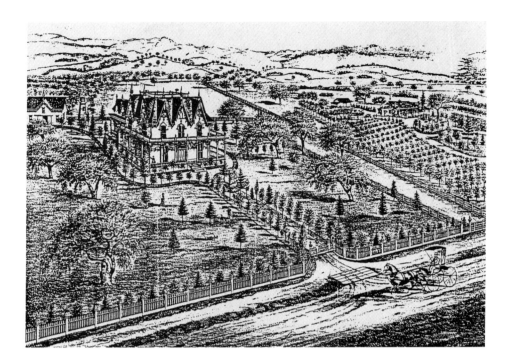

FIGURE 5
Artist unknown, *Res. of Mrs. SARAH WALLIS, Mayfield, Santa Clara Co. CAL*, source unidentified, ca. 1875, lithographic illustration *Private Collection*

Sarah's own character is a matter of some mystery. Eliza Gregson had noted a perhaps minor frailty (" . . . I fulfilled my part but she forgot her part"), but Talbot, in a letter to Thomas Larkin, dated September 21, 1853, suggested something of a much darker nature:

> [I married Mrs. Montgomery] from interest, knowing her former character well, but because she had a strong and determined character, much more so than my own, I thought it was my only salvation at the time. I really loved her although knowing what I did of her.[14]

And, in 1851, speaking of Sarah, George McKinstry Jr. wrote to an associate in San Diego: "I have not seen her for a long time but am told she's the same black bottle woman."[15]

Not one to be undone by either abandonment or betrayal, Sarah took in boarders until July 1854 and then married, this third time to Joseph S. Wallis, an attorney who became a judge and later a state senator. They acquired considerable wealth and, in 1856, purchased the 250-acre Mayfield Farm in Santa Clara County. They built a large, seven-gabled Gothic house and surrounded it with orchards (FIG. 5), and Sarah settled into a life of community activities, "taking part sometimes in public meetings of progressive and strong minded females"[16]; in 1870 she became president of the California Women's Suffrage Association.

Financial reversals in 1878 forced the sale of Mayfield Farm, and when Sarah died in 1905, at eighty-seven, it was in a small house purchased for her by her son. Did she dream, in those last years, of entertaining Susan B. Anthony in that gabled mansion or perhaps of the group of new Californians that were her guests in the pine woods on the American River at a "quilting" a half-century earlier?

NOTES

1. John Sutter et al., *New Helvetia Diary* (San Francisco: The Grabhorn Press in arrangement with The Society of California Pioneers, 1939), p. 25. During that year, the entries were made alternately by John Bidwell, at that time Chief Manager and bookkeeper at the fort, and William N. Loker, assistant manager. Since Mr. Loker was delivering those one hundred sheep on the twenty-ninth, the author of the entry would appear to be Mr. Bidwell.

2. Manuscript Collection, Box 285, Folder of Reading Collection, California Section, California State Library, Sacramento, Calif.

3. See Sandi Fox, *For Purpose and Pleasure: Quilting Together in Nineteenth-Century America* (Nashville, Tenn.: Rutledge Hill Press, 1995).

4. Two entries in *New Helvetia Diary* reference his work: November 28, 1845, "—Sent for the shingles that were at Mr. Montgomery's—" and March 28, 1846, "A Montgomery came and took away his anvil and his stake"; see Sutter, *New Helvetia Diary*, pp. 14, 29.

5. In addition to *New Helvetia Diary*, I have relied particularly on Hubert Howe Bancroft, *History of California* (San Francisco: The History Company, 1886).

6. Sutter, *New Helvetia Diary*, p. 21.

7. Eliza Marshall Gregson, "Mrs. Gregson's Memory," in "The Gregson Memoirs," *California Historical Quarterly* 19, no. 1 (1940): 118.

8. Kevin Jones, costume researcher, generously provided this careful interpretation of the object's construction. I am particularly grateful to Melani Wilkie, whose extended and determined search through the collections at Sutter's Fort brought this important dress to my attention, to this book, and to the exhibition.

9. Several sources have provided general information regarding Sarah's early years. Particularly helpful were Sally Garoutte, "California's First Quilting Party," *Uncoverings* (1981); "Sarah Montgomery Wallis," in Donovan Lewis, *Pioneers of California: True Stories of Early Settlers in the Golden State* (San Francisco: Scottwall Associates, 1993); Dorothy Regnery, "Pioneering Women," *The Californian: Magazine of the California History Center Foundation* 8, no. 2.

10. In 1846, a small vigilante group—settlers to California who were unhappy with the way California was governed—briefly captured Mexico's military base at Sonoma. Unbeknownst to them, the United States had declared war on Mexico earlier with the acquisition of California its main objective. After holding General Mariano Guadalupe Vallejo prisoner, the rebels raised a grizzly bear flag and declared war on Mexico; their goal was to make California a new, separate nation. The event, which came to be known as the Bear Flag Rebellion, is commemorated on the California State flag. See "California Statehood: New Economies and Opportunities," in *California History Guide* (Los Angeles: Natural History Museum of Los Angeles County, 2001), section C, pp. 1–2.

11. Gregson, "Mrs. Gregson's Memory," p. 121.

12. *California Pioneer Register and Index* (Baltimore, Md.: Regional Publishing Company, 1964), p. 251, excerpted from Bancroft, *History of California*.

13. See John Adam Hussey, "New Light upon Talbot H. Green," *California Historical Society Quarterly* 3 (1924): 32–63.

14. George P. Hammond, ed., *The Larkin Papers: Personal, Business and Official Correspondence of Thomas Oliver Larkin, Merchant and United States Consul in California*, vol. 3 (Berkeley and Los Angeles: University of California Press, 1952), p. 269.

15. George McKinstry Jr. to Edward M. Kern, San Diego, September 23, 1851, MS 122, Fort Sutter Papers, Huntington Library, San Marino, Calif. Historians are unclear as to the meaning of this phrase; could it refer to laudanum or alcohol?

16. *California Pioneer Register and Index*, p. 251.

PART 2

"A Small Tent, Two Old Quilts, Ten Pounds of Flour"

$\mathscr{T}$HE CONCEPT OF CALIFORNIA was shaped by the image makers—the publishers, the poets, the painters; their visions inspired those who journeyed as well as those who chose not to venture west to "see the elephant" for themselves. The mining camps of the popular press, for example, were populated with naughty rascals, but in the 1850s, a series of paintings of industrious miners suggested a trend toward social respectability.[1] Hubert Howe Bancroft, the early California historian, had reassured his readers of this eventuality:

> And so like boys escaped from school, from supervision, the adventurer yielded to the impulse, and allowed the spirit within him to run riot. . . .Among the general free and magnificent disorder, recklessness had its votaries, which led to . . . a full indulgence in exciting pastimes. All this, however, was but the bubble and spray of the river hurrying on to a grander and calmer future.[2]

In 1853, that "magnificent disorder" was reshaped by an artist, Henry Walton, into an orderly miner's cabin (FIG. 1). There is a blue-and-white one-patch quilt (or is it a comforter?) on the bunk-style bed. The painter may have intended it as a civilizing symbol there in the mining camp, Rough & Ready, and it may have reminded the miner, William Peck, of Mother and Home, but before symbolism and sentiment the quilt was there, quite simply, to keep him warm.

FIGURE 1
Henry Walton, *William D. Peck at Rough & Ready*, 1853, oil on board, 12 x 14 in. (30.5 x 35.6 cm)
Courtesy of the Oakland Museum of California

Quilts and comforters were indispensable to the journey west. *The Prairie Traveler*, published by the War Department in 1859, became one of the principal manuals used by the pioneers; it advised:

> The bedding for each person should consist of two blankets, a comforter, and a pillow, and a gutta percha or painted canvas cloth to spread beneath the bed upon the ground, and to contain it when rolled up for transportation.[3]

Many of the quilts brought west held sentimental recollections of the family of quilt-makers left behind—mothers and grandmothers, sisters and cousins and aunts. And on the travelers' departure, family and friends and neighbors often presented them with a friendship quilt, richly inscribed with names, biblical verses, and poetry, whose principal parting message was simply "remember me."

> *The gay Savannah's of the West,*
> *Are soon to be thy home,*
> *That dear wild bird we loved so well*
> *Will from us widely roam*
> *But when at night you bend the knee*
> *Unto your childhood's God*
> *Oh! let us then remembered be*
> *Whose name we here record.*[4]

But quilts joined the journey mainly as functional objects. In recording their presence on the trail, diaries and journals almost always spoke of them quite unemotionally, and without descriptive text.

> Last night when traveling, I had to wrap a quilt around me and I seen some of the men with overcoats on.
> —VIOLA SPRINGER, 1885

> As it had rained up to this time our quilts were soaking wet. I hung them on a fence soon they were frozen stiff I had to dry our quilts around the camp fire till 12 oclock.
> —ANNA HANSBERRY, 1903

> I have spent the day writing home, tonight I'm setting with a bed quilt around my chest, hat on my head playing dice with Fred. Such is western life. Wouldn't the Whitewater falks stare in aghast.
> —ADA COLVIN, 1870[5]

John Hess and his wife had, at the direction of Brigham Young, joined those men leaving the main body of the Mormon migration to travel with the Mormon battalion toward California. When he left *that* weary company, he remembered:

> I was now in a country that was untried and one thousand miles from where any supplies could be got with only the outfit of a discharged soldier…a small tent…two old quilts, ten pounds of flour and my dear wife Emeline who had been with me through all the trials and hardships and had endured them all without a murmur.[6]

As early quilts moved from one generation to the next, it was believed that many had been worked on the trail to California, but the actual number of these is probably quite small. Although a few of the wealthier families traveled west with more than one wagon, and at least a few of those were outfitted in the back as a small sitting room, this was the great exception. The wagons were crowded with goods and supplies and women spent a great deal of time walking beside them; domestic activities took up most of their time when the wagons stopped. We know, however, that several quiltmakers had prepared packets of small, precut fabric pieces to sew into blocks as they traveled.

In Illinois, in the winter before she and her family left for California, Mary Margaret Hezlep, her paternal grandmother, and her aunt began assembling fabric for the "Road to California" quilt Mary intended to work on the trip. More than thirty members of the wagon train (from Iowa, Illinois, and Ohio) inscribed the blocks: "Left Hamilton, April 15, 1859," "Seven months on the road," "Crossed the Plains," "Ho for California." Mary was fifteen years old when they arrived in California in 1859, but she did not assemble her nine-patch blocks until 1884, when she presented the quilt to her fourteen-year-old daughter.[7]

By the time the settlers came west, the major techniques and stylistic directions of America's quilts had been set; once they arrived in California, American quiltmakers simply rethreaded their needles and continued to pursue their pleasure.

NOTES

1. Claire Perry, *Pacifica Arcadia: Images of California 1600–1915* (New York and Oxford: Oxford University Press, 1999), p. 48.
2. Hubert Howe Bancroft, *History of California*, vol. 6, 1848–1859 (San Francisco: The History Company, 1888), p. 226.
3. Captain Randolph B. Marcy, *The Prairie Traveler: A Hand-book for Overland Expeditions* (Washington, D.C.: War Department, 1859), p. 40.
4. Inscribed on the *Hoagland Quilt* (New Jersey, 1855), collection of the Los Angeles County Museum of Art, gift of Herb Wallerstein. Illustrated and discussed in Sandi Fox, *For Purpose and Pleasure: Quilting Together in Nineteenth-Century America* (Nashville, Tenn.: Rutledge Hill Press, 1995), pp. 136–41.
5. Kenneth L. Holmes, ed., *Covered Wagon Women: Diaries & Letters from the Western Trails, 1840–1890*, vol. 11 (Glendale, Calif. and Spokane, Wash.: The Arthur H. Clark Company, 1993), pp. 51, 126, 171.
6. John R. Young, "Reminiscences of John R. Young," *Utah Historical Quarterly* 3 (1930): 53.
7. Illustrated in Jean Ray Laury and the California Heritage Quilt Project, *Ho for California! Pioneer Women and Their Quilts* (New York: E. P. Dutton, 1990), pp. 43–46.

THE "STARS AND SWAGS" QUILT

Kentucky, ca. 1855
Quiltmaker unidentified
Cotton; pieced, appliquéd, embroidered, and quilted
86⅜ x 85⅞ in. (220 x 218 cm)
California State Parks, Sutter's Fort

THIS VIBRANT QUILT WAS "pieced by grandmother" before her great adventure began, and it traveled across the continent to California in 1860, arriving safely to become a treasured addition to the state's historical textiles. The pieced stars and appliquéd swags (FIG. 1) that were so wonderfully worked in Kentucky would be duplicated in California in endless variations; embroidery would continue to embellish cleverly contrived buds and leaves (FIG. 2); and small, even, quilted stitches would continue to create whole new secondary patterns over all.

It is in many ways remarkable that this Kentucky quilt, and so many others, survived the harshness of the trail. Paintings and pianos and porcelain often had to be left to that easier life, or abandoned to the terrible land that exhausted men, women, and oxen were trying to cross. But quilts, creative or common, were carefully folded and packed in wagons that must of first importance hold the necessities for survival. That the quilts could keep her family warm was the quiltmaker's justification for those precious few inches of space. It was, in the end, that simple need for warmth that carried the craft across the continent.

The *"Stars and Swags"* Quilt

THE SHIP *BROOKLYN* QUILT

New York, ca. 1845
Made by Catherine Crast Sloat
for Sarah Sloat Burr
Cotton; pieced and quilted
84 x 74 in. (213.4 x 188 cm)
Collection of the Waters family

FROM THE FRONT PORCH of their farmhouse near Port Leyden, New York, about a mile from the river, Nathan and Chloe Burr could look east across the densely wooded Black River Valley to the Adirondack Mountains. The farm was large: crops and animals, barns and buildings, and an orchard to the southwest.[1] Yet in 1846 they were moved to leave this tranquil setting to set sail for California. Their son Amasa would travel with them, as would a second son, Charles Clark Burr, with his wife, Sarah Sloat Burr, and their young son. Although it is unclear how many of the family were members of the Church of Jesus Christ of Latter-Day Saints,[2] it was with the Mormons that they moved west.

In 1845, the Church was expelled from Nauvoo, Illinois, and its leader, Brigham Young, prepared to lead the "Saints" overland to establish Zion in the West; he selected Samuel Brannan, a twenty-seven-year-old printer, to lead a group of Mormons ahead to California by ship.

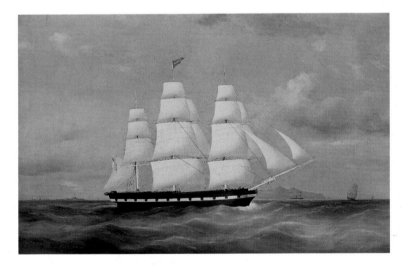

We have chartered the ship *Brooklyn* [FIG. I] under Captain Richardson. . . .She is a first class ship in the best of order for sea and, with all the rest, a first class, very fast sailer, which will facilitate our passage greatly . . . very neatly fitted up . . . to make a family equally as comfortable as by their own fire side.[3]

The fare for each adult was set at $50 and for each child at $25. Twenty-five dollars per person would be charged for provisions. When the ship sailed, on February 4, 1846, seventy men, sixty-eight women, and one hundred children were on the passenger list.

Although fraught with danger and discomfort, one advantage of a sea voyage was that many articles too cumbersome to take by land could be accommodated; Brannan was directed to take with him all materials necessary to establish a self-sustaining community of about eight hundred Mormons. (Although it was not to occur, it was expected that the overland emigration would join the seaborne contingent in California.) The cargo was vast and varied, including a printing press and a two-year supply of paper and ink, sawmills and flouring mills, saddles and sewing machines, seeds and plows and harrows, a library of 179 books, medicine, and enough food for seven months. They also

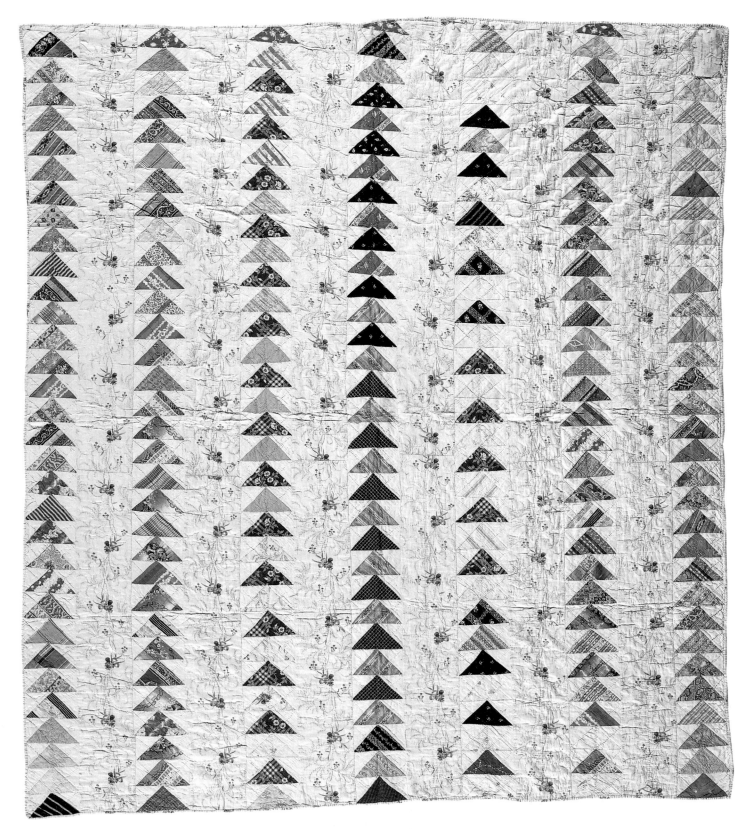

The Ship Brooklyn *Quilt*

carried with them two milk cows, forty pigs, and a crate of fowl. Indeed, a sailor unloading it all recorded it as

> the most heterogeneous mass of materials ever crowded together; in fact it seemed as if, like the ship of Noah, it contained a representative of every mortal thing the mind of man had ever conceived.[4]

Nathan and Chloe and Charles and Sarah sold their farms in January 1846, scant weeks before they set sail. We cannot imagine what of their eastern life they selected to take with them, but we do know of one item, a quilt that had been made for Sarah by her mother, Catherine Crast Sloat (1798–1873). Family history identifies the quilt (FIG. 2) as part of Sarah's trousseau (she was married on December 28, 1843), but the quilt itself is of rather enigmatic construction, with an older, faded, pieced quilt on its reverse (FIG. 3).

Catherine (Caty) was born in Albany, New York, as the eighteenth century came to a close, and she married John Lounsbury Sloat in 1818; their eleven children were all born in Jefferson, Schoharie County, New York. Sarah was the only child to leave New York, and although she had gone west to settle with the Mormons, the virulent anti-Mormon attitudes of the period do not seem to have caused a breach with the family; according to a census report, Catherine could neither read nor write but Sarah corresponded frequently with her father and her siblings.[5]

The accommodations aboard the *Brooklyn* were hardly as Brannan had described them. The relatively small square-rigger was, in fact, a "tired merchantman" and the "staterooms" prepared for that six-month journey were small, dark, damp, and dreary. The beds were wooden bunks with straw mattresses. Fearful storms wracked the vessel. In the midst of all, Sarah (eight months pregnant when the voyage commenced) delivered her second son; he was appropriately named John Atlantic Burr (a second child born on board was named Georgiana Pacific Robbins).

Less than a month after John's birth, Sarah's firstborn (named Charles after his father) died of dysentery; he had not yet reached his second birthday. He "was buried in the Atlantic Ocean being strapped to a board, wrapped in blankets and weighted with a flat iron." At least three other infants had died just before Charles; when little John Franklin died, "They tenderly wrapped him in quilts, weighted his little body and laid it to rest at the bottom of the mighty Atlantic."[6]

The story of the voyage of the *Brooklyn* is one with complicated religious and political implications, and it is widely documented. On July 31, 1846, when the ship sailed at last into the harbor at Yerba Buena (named for the

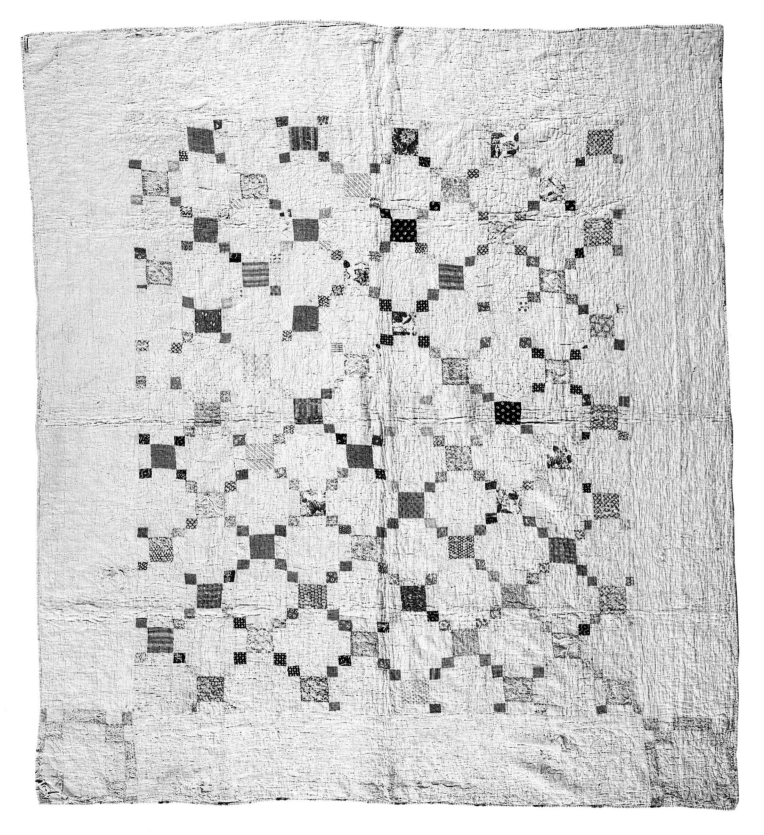

FIGURE 3
The Ship Brooklyn *Quilt*, reverse

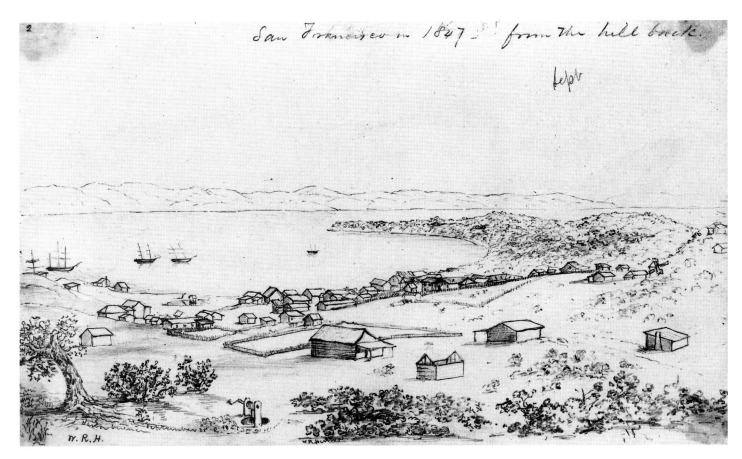

San Francisco in 1847 from the hill back.

Sept

FIGURE 4
William Rich Hutton (1826–1901),
*San Francisco, View of Yerba Buena,
1847*, 1847, pencil drawing, 5¾ x 9⅟₁₆
in. (14 x 23 cm) *Reproduced by
permission of the Huntington Library, San
Marino, California*

NOTES

1. Wesley R. Burr, and Ruth J. Burr, *A History
    of the Burr Pioneers* (Provo, Utah: The
    Charles and Sarah Burr Family Organiza-
    tion, 1995), p. 43.
2. Family history suggests that Charles was a
    member of the Church but that Sarah was
    not.
3. Sam Brannan, *The Messenger*, December 15,
    1845.
4. Burr et al., *A History*, p. 45.
5. Ibid., p. 117.
6. Ibid., p. 51.
7. Sarah Burr's diaries are in the Historical
    Department of the Church of Jesus Christ
    of Latter-Day Saints in Salt Lake City. I am
    grateful to the library staff for their kind
    assistance, and for permission to reproduce
    and to quote.

peppermint that was plentiful around some local springs; later San Francisco) (FIG. 4), Sam Brannan saw the American flag flying. He was bitterly disap-pointed, as he had hoped to be the first to raise it. The local population was very small and when the travelers disembarked Yerba Buena became, for a time, a Mormon community.

Sarah had other children (FIG. 5); she lived sixty years as a wife and seven years as a widow. At least eleven of her later diaries have survived, recording the ordinary daily life of a woman who had taken a historic journey. Making brief entries in small, unmatched volumes (FIG. 6), she marked her domestic duties ("a washing wool," "a churning") and her social events ("relief society dance," "Had for my birthday all the grandchildren to dinner there was 19 of them"). She found it "Pleasant a sewing rags," and six months later she "made my carpet." There were frequent diversions: "Got my likeness taken," "The dog killed the chicks." She complained frequently of headaches. And as her mother had before her, Sarah Sloat Burr made quilts.

> I got a quilt on.
> Sister Beal Amelia Cara [and] Laura quilted it off.[7]

THE "BUDS AND LEAVES" QUILT

San Francisco, California, ca. 1855
Made by Rosina Catherine Elizabeth Hummel Widman
Cotton; appliquéd, embroidered, and
quilted; inked inscription
81 x 80 in. (205.7 x 203.2 cm)
Collection of Mildred Breitbarth and Linda Breitbarth

IN 1850, ONLY SIXTEEN YEARS OLD and barely a bride, Rosina Catherine Widman prepared for a sea voyage, the second in her young life. Orphaned in Germany at age nine, she had immigrated to Ohio with her aunt and uncle and now she and her husband, William Fredrick (FIGS. 1 and 2) had determined to move to California. Were they propelled by the same aspirations that drove Benjamin Carpenter to leave his Clinton, Missouri, home in 1849?

> My object in going to California is to get a sufficient amount of money to allow
> me to furnish and fit a suitable home for myself and [Jane]. And have a sufficient
> amount of capital to allow me to engage in some business which with ordinary
> success would bring proffits sufficient to keep myself and those dependent on me
> in reasonably good living and to allow us to pass in good society for the time now
> has come when industrious poverty is no passport in society.[1]

Could Rosina and William have hoped for more?

Like Benjamin, they elected the fastest route, across the Isthmus of Panama, for how long would the gold and the fortunes last? The overland journey was not an option for the most eager of argonauts; although the trail had been opened and crossed, it could not be traveled until late April or early May,

FIGURE 1
William Fredrick Widman, undated
photograph

FIGURE 2
Rosina Catherine Widman and her son,
San Francisco, ca. 1855, daguerreotype,
photographer unidentified

and they would not reach California before August or September, at best. By sea, once the decision was made, travel could begin at once. The journey around Cape Horn was an established route—and it proved to be the most popular during the first frenzied year of the rush for gold—but it took five to eight months to complete. Crossing the Isthmus reduced the time to six to eight weeks—sailing from New York to the mouth of the Chagres River, transferring to mules for the trip through twenty-six miles of dense jungle, crossing the Isthmus to Panama City and the Pacific Ocean, and then catching another vessel to San Francisco. Although traversing the Isthmus was the shortest of the three major routes to California, the traveler was led to expect peril and pestilence.[2]

The "Buds and Leaves" Quilt

Rosina left no known journals. Perhaps, like Margaret De Witt, she ignored the possibility of danger, anticipating that "...if it is not too warm, it will be fine fun—sailing and riding the Donkeys."[3] Perhaps, as did Mary Ballou, she found a harsher reality; in her Chagres hotel Mary wrote:

> [there was] no floor but the ground for my bed a valiece for my pillow a hard bed indeed. I wept bitterly. there were twenty five in our company all Laid on the ground. the monkeys were howling the Nighthawks were singing the natives were watching.[4]

And when she was faced with the terrifying mule path: "part the way I walked Part the way I rode and part the way I Laught and part the way I wept."[5] This was the path that Rosina crossed, that Jennie Megquier described as "nothing but a path wide enough for the feet of the mule, which if he would make a misstep you would go to parts unknown...."[6] But many of the women who crossed the Isthmus were absolutely delighted with the lush foliage, the parrots, and the brilliant flowers, and absent her own words, we can only hope it was so for Rosina.

In 1849, Isaac W. Baker of Massachusetts, traveling on the mule path, sketched an incident on the Chagres (FIG. 3); that his fellow traveler was a woman was indeed an "incident" worthy of note. Although it was the fashion to ride sidesaddle, the difficult trail led many of the ladies to ride astride, as here, wearing men's trousers. The rider is otherwise fashionably attired in bonnet and gown.

While others made entries in their diaries, and with no children to watch over, Rosina and William occupied their time at sea with a task they had devised in Ohio before their departure. Among their belongings they had packed an amount of red and green fabric and a white cotton ground sufficient to produce a quilt. The accoutrements they tucked into Rosina's little leather sewing kit were small and few (FIG. 4); they included the pencil with which William marked the floral components he then cut out for his young bride to sew and the tiny knife with which he sharpened it. The technical requirements of an appliqué quilt make it an unlikely choice for a journey's diversion, but the story of the quilt and its origins seems to have been confirmed years later to Rosina's granddaughter by a woman who was a young child on the same voyage. The quilt was finished in San Francisco, where Rosina and William's journey ended and where they made their home. The buds on each of the nine stylized wreaths and on the undulating vine borders (FIG. 5) were embellished

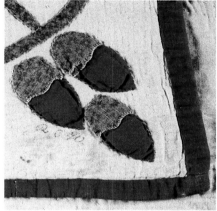

FIGURE 5, LEFT
The "Buds and Leaves" Quilt (detail)

FIGURE 6, ABOVE
The "Buds and Leaves" Quilt (detail)

with a bit of embroidery, and in a corner, Rosina wrote her initials, "RCW," in small, now-faded script (FIG. 6).[7]

The 1852 city directory listed Rosina as a dressmaker; she and William would have two sons and two daughters. Mary Ballou, Margaret De Witt, and Jennie Megquier seem to have slipped into anonymous domesticity. And what of Benjamin Carpenter? The future with Jane (the "suitable home," the entry into "good society") was never realized. In Missouri, it was announced at a meeting of his Masonic Lodge that letters from California had advised his family of his death there, just eleven months after the initial entry in his travel journal.

NOTES

1. Benjamin Carpenter, "Ben Carpenter's Sayings and Doings," 1849–50, unpublished manuscript, Autry Museum of Western Heritage, Los Angeles, p. 1.
2. As on the overland trail, the travelers' great fear was cholera. Mr. and Mrs. William Ferguson had seen it take twenty-eight of their shipmates, and on the Isthmus it took William. His wife buried him under a mahogany tree at a spot called the American Burying Grounds; see Jo Ann Levy, *They Saw the Elephant: Women in the California Gold Rush* (Norman: University of Oklahoma Press, 1992), p. 173.
3. Margaret De Witt, De Witt Family Papers, the Bancroft Library, University of California, Berkeley.
4. Quoted in Levy, *They Saw the Elephant*, p. 34.
5. Ibid., p. 41.
6. Ibid.
7. Carpenter, "Ben Carpenter's Sayings and Doings," loose page in the journal.

ELSIE ANN BURR'S QUILT

Fairfield, Illinois, marked 1849
Made by Elsie Ann Burr
83 x 67 in. (210.8 x 170.2 cm)
Cotton; pieced, embroidered, and quilted
Los Angeles County Museum of Art;
gift of Patricia (Mrs. Jackson) Edwards

"MOVING WEST" WAS USUALLY AN INCREMENTAL UNDERTAKING. In 1836, when Atwell and Betsey Wheeler Burr left Pompey, New York, with their nine children, their sights were set only as far as Illinois. Their daughter, Elsie Ann Burr (born 1824), was almost twelve years old when she said good-bye to the people and places of her girlhood. In 1849, when she was twenty-five years old, she returned to upper New York State for a sentimental visit; while there, she requested a bit of fabric from each of those she visited, determined to construct a quilt upon her return to Illinois commemorating those treasured friendships.

The pieced pattern she chose was popular and practical; she could enter the names on the muslin strip in the center of each block in the cross-stitches she had perfected on a sampler she had worked in Pompey in 1835, "Wrought in the 11th year of her age." She marked a block each for "Little Flora D.," cousins Betsey, Elnora, Frizah, and Sarah Ann in Pompey; and Aunt Unita and cousins Frances and Lovantia in DeRuyter. The names on the quilt, including her own, would eventually number forty from more than a dozen of the small New York villages she had visited.[1]

Each cross-stitched name and village is placed off to the right of each center strip; this rather odd placement can be explained by one particular block marked "Cousin S. Lavonia R. / DeRuyter" (FIG. 1). Here to the left, in a space left blank on the other strips, is a secondary inscription, "Died March 5th 49 / Aged 18. / She lives again / in Heaven." The quilt Elsie Ann called her album quilt has thus become a mourning quilt as well, the other names eventually to be accompanied by the dates of an inevitable death. It may have been intended as a mourning quilt from the beginning; did Lavonia's death, in 1849, occur during Elsie Ann's visit to New York?

Early deaths and elaborate mourning rituals were particular to the period; six years earlier a young Elsie Ann had

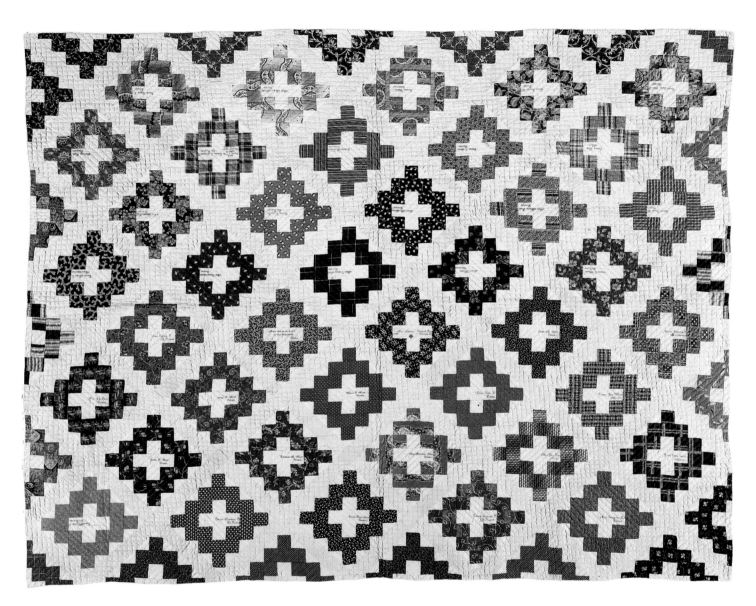

Elsie Ann Burr's Quilt

FIGURE 2
The Frank Burr house, Monrovia,
California, ca. 1893 *Courtesy of Monrovia
Historical Society*

produced another mourning tribute to yet another cousin: "LINES, / Composed on the Death of DANIEL WARNE / who died January 7th, 1843, in the / twenty-fourth year of his age." From the nine four-line verses:

> *Ye weeping friends with me draw near,*
> *And pause o'er him who slumbers here,*
> *Though cold his form beneath the sod,*
> *His spirit winged its way to God.*
>
> *By all beloved—in prime of life,*
> *What though his thoughts with hope were rife,*
> *Consumption came, and none could save*
> *Its victim from an early grave. . . .*[2]

Elsie Ann never married, and when she died is unclear. We do know that she and her older sister, Gerdentia, raised their nephew, Frank, whose mother died only a few weeks after his birth. In 1889, Frank and his family and Gerdentia (Aunt Den) moved to Monrovia, California. In 1893 the family and two unidentified visitors posed in front of their new house on 150 North Myrtle (FIG. 2). In the photograph, Mollie, the family horse with the distinctive white

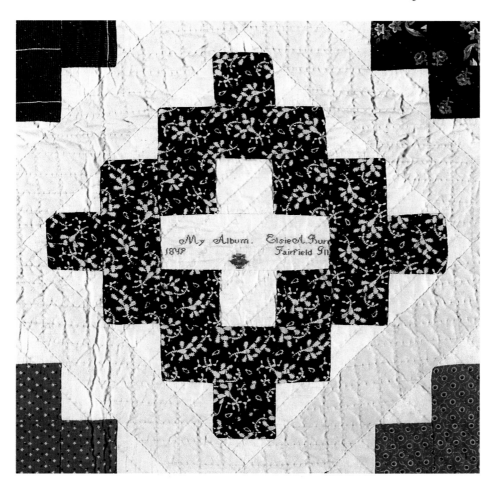

FIGURE 3
Elsie Ann Burr's Quilt (detail)

blaze, stands with the carriage to the far right. Mr. and Mrs. Burr (Frank and Laura) are present, of course, with Aunt Den and their five children—Walter, Jay Lester, and Myron, and sitting on the steps, always together, Clyde and little Gladys Mae. Elsie Ann's album quilt (FIG. 3) had found a new home at the foot of the San Gabriel Mountains.

NOTES

1. The New York villages entered on the quilt are: Camillus, Cazenovia, DeRuyter, Ellington, Lisle, Nelson, Norwich, Oxford, Pitcher, Pompey, Preston, Sempronius, and Woodstock. Two cousins from "Massachusetts" were included.
2. The published source is unidentified.

MARY ALLEN'S QUILT

Pennsylvania and New Jersey, marked 1847
Made by Mary Pancoast Allen
Cotton; pieced, appliquéd, embroidered, and quilted;
inked inscriptions and drawings
89 x 117 in. (226.1 x 297.2 cm)
Los Angeles County Museum of Art; gift of Pam Ferris

IN THE EARLY 1840S, in the Delaware Valley, and particularly among The Religious Society of Friends, the Quakers, signature quilts began to appear in substantial numbers. A few within the group are of particular distinction in both design and execution; such is the quilt made by Mary Pancoast Allen (born 1819). The large surface with its cutout corners was meant to accommodate a four-post bed; it was a space sufficient to hold the large number of inscriptions that recorded a family's collective memory.

In contrast to the simplicity of the pieced blocks that dominate the quilt's surface, the central block of Mary's quilt (FIG. 1) is an intricately worked floral

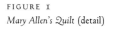

FIGURE 1
Mary Allen's Quilt (detail)

Mary Allen's Quilt

motif: a pieced and appliquéd wreath surrounded by four sprays of green printed velvet leaves, four small buds, and wispy inked tendrils. The appliquéd edges are embellished with an outlining embroidery stitch. In the center, an inked, floral, open spray delicately embraces the quiltmaker's inked inscription of authorship and intent:

10th Mo 1847
Mary P Allen
I will not mourn my griefs below
Nor all their baneful train
But hope at last to meet above
My early Friends again.

The pieced blocks represent a large collection of red and yellow cotton prints, but it is the inscribed muslin strips separating those blocks that merits our closest attention. There are numerous mourning references: "Father! Mother! Though no more / Meet me on this earthly shore"; "Wilt thou sweet mourner at my grave appear / and soothe my spirit lingering near / Say when taken from this world and me / I lay my head beneath the willow tree." But the muslin strips in most instances contain the names of family and friends, as well as the sentimental confirmations of friendship one would expect to find on the pages of a friendship/autograph book of the period:

When 'neath this quilt thy form reclines
Please think of him who penned these lines.

Remember me, whilst life shall be
A source of happiness to thee.

Forget me not—Forget me not
A frequent wish that's seldom got.

Remember me as life is sweet
Remember me 'til next we meet.

Yet this one boon I ask of thee,
It is "Forget me not,"
Happy mayst though ever be
And peaceful be thy lot.

Over eighty names appear on the quilt representing thirty-one families.[1] Many strips also contain a geographical identification and many are dated, written in the Quaker manner: "Lydia White / Penn's Neck 7th Mo 10th 1846." The earliest date is 1841. Significantly, where slight staining appears on several of the strips, it does not extend into the adjoining blocks, indicating that the strips and blocks were set together at a later time.

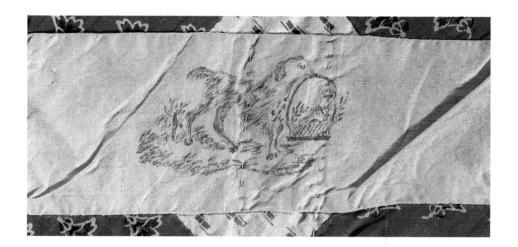

FIGURE 2
Mary Allen's Quilt (detail)

The strips also provide the small canvases for a large number of tiny sketches, including a dog carrying a cat in a basket (FIG. 2); a saw, hammer, T square, and compass; a plow and a sheaf of wheat; acorns and oak leaves and baskets of flowers; roses and ribbons; and a full-mast sailing vessel (FIG. 3).

The quilt would serve Mary Allen's descendants well as they moved with it, eventually to California—names and dates captured on cloth when memory had faded.

NOTE

1. The family names are: Allen, Appleton, Bassett, Bradway, Brown, Buckingham, Carpenter, Colson, Dunn, Fillcraft, Gillingham, Glasskill, Green, Hall, Hance, Hancock, Hilliard, Lippincott, Lester, Moore, Pancoast, Parker, Petite, Pickering, Prakett, Reyser, Roberts, Sailer, Silver, Watson, and White.

FIGURE 3
Mary Allen's Quilt (detail)

THE BOARDMAN QUILT

Philadelphia, Pennsylvania, marked 1843
Made for Reverend and Mrs. George S. Boardman
by the Ladies of the Third Presbyterian Church
Cotton; appliquéd, embroidered, and quilted;
inked inscriptions and sketches
105⅝ x 120½ in. (268.3 x 306.1 cm)
Los Angeles County Museum of Art, purchased with funds
provided by the Don Benito Chapter of the Questers;
partial gift of Dolores B. Thomas

FIGURE 1
The Boardman Quilt (detail)

IN 1819, OHIO AND KENTUCKY were considered the Far West, where for two years Reverend George S. Boardman rode on horseback preaching the Presbyterian gospel. In 1821 he was installed in the church at Watertown, New York, beginning a "precious and fruitful pastorate" of sixteen years' duration. Following pastoral assignments in Rochester, New York, and Columbus, Ohio, he spent a brief year in Philadelphia at the Third Presbyterian Church, more informally referred to as the Old Pine Street Church. In those twelve months his impact on his Philadelphia congregation must have been considerable, for when he left to take charge of the Second Church in Rome, New York, he and his wife were presented with this quilt of exceptional excellence. Beneath the flower-filled urn that dominates the quilt's central block, a steady hand inscribed "Presented / to the / Revd. George S. & Sarah Boardman / by the Ladies of the / Third Presbyterian Church / of Philadelphia / 1843" (FIG. 1). Above the urn, just inside the top curve of the floral wreath that surrounds it, is inscribed "How beautiful upon the mountains are the feet of Him that bringeth good tidings."

The names on nineteenth-century album quilts were scribed and stenciled, stamped and stitched, and many (as on the *Boardman Quilt*) included a brief phrase or verse, usually a mix of religion and nineteenth-century sentimentality. Pamelia Adeline Higerood, for example, wrote "O be each flower a book, where we may see / Dear records of Religion and of Thee / And may all nature move / Thoughts of thy matchless love." In the first line of

The Boardman Quilt

her chosen verse, Pamelia had, in fact, captured the essence of this quilt; each of the 101 blocks that surround the central medallion may be seen as a page in a glorious autograph book, all written in the "language of flowers" (FIG. 2).

It is obvious that several of the imported chintz fabrics used on the quilt were shared by the ladies; certain identical sprays appear on several blocks. In three instances, the same fabric provided motifs for seven blocks. Of particular interest is the spray of moss roses and buds (FIG. 3) that provided the illustration for eight blocks. The flower itself was a great favorite in simple country gardens (its popularity would peak in 1850–60), and this particular fabric was evidently a great favorite in Philadelphia, where it was used often on a segment of similar friendship and album quilts worked during this period. It is included, for example, on an album quilt made by Sarah Flickwir; its surface arrangement (blocks surrounding a central medallion of a wreath-enclosed floral motif) closely resembles that of the *Boardman Quilt*. Another chintz appears frequently: a peacock perched on a flower-based pedestal is found on six blocks of the *Boardman Quilt*, on Sarah's quilt, and on a quilt attributed to the members of the Sewing Society of the First Baptist Church.[1]

In addition to a common use of textiles, there were a number of threads that bound together a group of highly sophisticated Philadelphia quilts, of which the three mentioned above are highly refined examples. The shared technique, cutout chintz appliquéd to a plain ground, is often referred to as

FIGURE 2
The Boardman Quilt (detail)

broderie perse, with the edges of the motifs occasionally secured and/or embellished with a small buttonhole stitch. No very early contemporaneous descriptions or details of *broderie perse* have come to light, but *The Ladies Hand Book of Fancy and Ornamental Work*, published in Philadelphia a decade after these quilts were worked, suggests the technique's continuing popularity:

> She cut squares of white, about a foot square, and in the centre of those she sewed down bunches of flowers, cut out very neatly from the high colored furniture chintz . . . and the effect was very beautiful.[2]

The pieces are all finely quilted, often in a variety of patterns; the *Boardman Quilt* includes straight, diagonal, and clamshell designs. And once completed, these album quilts were presented to a favored few. There was a tradition of such quilts in the Sewing Society of the First Baptist Church of Philadelphia (and perhaps among the Ladies of the Third Presbyterian Church as well), and one was presented in 1846 to Sister Deborah Wade of the Karen Mission in Burma:

> permit me in behalf of the Sisters of the Sewing Society, to present for your acceptance, an Album bedquilt.—Inscribed on it you will find when you have leisure to examine it many precious promises from the word of life, and sentiments warm from Christian hearts. Receive it, as it is intended, not from any value in itself, but as a small token of affection, for the Master's sake, and the high estimation in which you are regarded by us—When our humble names appear before you Pray for us.[3]

Eighteen hundred and forty-three—the year those eastern ladies were preoccupied with bits of glazed chintz on their elaborate tribute to Reverend Boardman—was the year in which the women of the Chiles-Walker Party of emigrants struggled across the Sierra Nevadas into California, concerned with the condition of wools and common calicoes that comprised their now-worn traveling clothes. It is that general westward path that the *Boardman Quilt* would take in the century to follow, but by that time the memories of Reverend Boardman would fade, and the details of his later life vanish, as the quilt passed to ever more distant descendants.

FIGURE 3
The Boardman Quilt (detail)

NOTES

1. The Sewing Society Quilt and Sarah Flickwir's album quilt are in the collection of the Philadelphia Museum of Art. Both are illustrated and discussed in the exhibition catalogue for *As Pieces Here to Pieces Join: American Appliqué Quilts, 1800–1900*, in Dilys Blum and Jack L. Lindsey, "Nineteenth-Century Appliqué Quilts," *Philadelphia Museum of Art Bulletin* 85, nos. 363, 364 (Fall 1989): 22–23ff.
2. Florence Hartley, *The Ladies Hand Book of Fancy and Ornamental Work* (Philadelphia: J. W. Bradley, 1861), p. 193.
3. "Minutes of the Female Missionary Society of the First Baptist Church of Philadelphia," collection of the church, in Blum and Lindsey, "Nineteenth-Century Appliqué Quilts," p. 28. The letter was written to Sister Wade by Ann Rhees, first director of the missionary society.

THE SCOTT/ORRICK QUAKER QUILT

Baltimore, Maryland, ca. 1847
Made for John and Elizabeth Littig Scott
Cotton; appliquéd, quilted, and embroidered;
inked inscriptions
90 x 88 in. (228.6 x 223.5 cm)
Collection of a member, American Decorative Arts Forum
of Northern California

FIGURE I
The Scott/Orrick Quaker Quilt (detail)

THE CLARITY OF PURPOSE INSCRIBED ON the *Boardman Quilt* ("Presented / to the / Revd. George S. & Sarah Boardman / by the Ladies of the / Third Presbyterian Church / of Philadelphia / 1843") is not present on this Baltimore quilt given to John and Elizabeth Littig Scott. It could not have been made to celebrate their marriage, as that had occurred in 1820. The earliest inscribed blocks were signed in 1845, closer to the 1844 birth of their daughter, Mary Frances, and it was through her that the quilt descended—as was often the case, from mothers to daughters.

Ten of the quilt's blocks were signed in ink—some printed and others in graceful script—and all have faded with time.[1] Three of the signators are Scotts (Mary M., E. A., E. B.) and may be presumed to be relatives; others may be kin as well, now identified with a husband's name. Anna Maria Harrison and Florence Murray each contributed a block; on Sarah Hodgson's Wilmington-worked block is a biblical reference to "Numbers / 6th Chapter / 24th / 25th. 26th. Ver."

The earliest marked blocks were, interestingly, signed within days of each other: Maria Crawford signed her block in Baltimore on February 5, 1845, four days after the offering by Elizabeth B. Hopkins. Elizabeth's block (FIG. I), central on the quilt, is the most elaborately inscribed:

> *Cast thy bread upon the waters: for thou*
> *shall find it after many days XI Eccl*
> *Elizabeth B. Hopkins*
> *Baltimore*
> *2d Month 1st 1845*

The manner in which Elizabeth Hopkins dated her work indicates its Quaker origins. If she herself worked the block she signed,[2] it attests to the

The Scott/Orrick Quaker Quilt

FIGURE 2
The Scott/Orrick Quaker Quilt (detail)

FIGURE 3
The Scott/Orrick Quaker Quilt (detail)

quality of her needlework, as her life attests to the quality of her character. Born in Maryland in 1804, she was thirty-three years old when she embraced the principles of that religious society; she spent the rest of her life in service to others. She served as matron at Haverford College and at the Maryland State Asylum for the Insane.

At least two extant quilts are firmly documented as having been made by inmates in nineteenth-century asylums. In 1850 a unique figurative quilt was worked by an inmate in the Spring Grove State Hospital in Catonsville, Maryland,[3] and a vibrant starburst quilt was pieced, ca. 1880, by inmates in the Salt Lake City Insane Asylum.[4] Did Elizabeth Hopkins transmit any of her quilt-making skills to those troubled souls in her care?

An unmarried Quaker, Elizabeth died in Zanesville, Ohio, at ninety-seven years of age; she had, indeed, "cast her bread upon the water."

Another signator, "Edith Dawson / Easton Md. / 1847," was eulogized as a woman of equal piety: "This dear Friend, with a meek and quiet spirit, was concerned to maintain the doctrines and testimonies of our religious Society through much privation and trial."[5] The 1850 Easton census recorded that Edith had a daughter who shared her name and would have been fifteen years old in 1847; although old enough to quilt, it is doubtful that she would have worked a block of this sophistication or that she, and not her mother, would have been working with quiltmakers of her mother's age.

FIGURE 4
The Scott/Orrick Quaker Quilt (detail)

By the 1840s, roller-printed English chintz was imported into Baltimore in substantial amounts, and these richly colored furnishing fabrics provided the floral motifs used on twenty-one of the blocks (FIG. 2); the edges of the wreaths and sprays on twelve of those were enhanced by tiny buttonhole stitches worked in silk thread (FIG. 3). The classic Baltimore album quilts were worked during the same period, primarily within the circle of Methodism, and four of the blocks on this quilt, appliquéd in red and green cotton calico, are drawn from that stylistic tradition. Mary B. Matthews's name (written on an inked ribbon floating atop an inked spray of leaves) appears at the center of one of those blocks (FIG. 4). Her name also appears on a Maryland quilt made in 1847 for a Methodist minister,[6] as does the name Orrick (it was not uncommon for a group of quiltmakers to reach outside of their own religious inclinations to complete their sewing circle).

In the 1870s, Mary Frances Scott Orrick and her husband, Oliver Summerfield Orrick, an attorney, departed for Oakland, California, her girlhood legacy carefully packed for the journey.

NOTES

1. The signatures are those of Mary B. Matthews, Sarah Hodgson, Mary M. Scott, Anna Maria Harrison, Elizabeth B. Hopkins, E. A. Scott, Edith Dawson, Florence Murray, E. B. Scott, and Maria Crawford.

2. Current and continuing research on friendship and album quilts indicates that when required—due to a lack of time or talent—elegant appliquéd quilt blocks could be purchased from professional needle workers.

3. For text and illustrations see Sandi Fox, *Wrapped in Glory: Figurative Quilts and Bedcovers 1700–1900* (New York and London: Los Angeles County Museum of Art and Thames and Hudson, 1990), pp. 76–79.

4. Illustrated and extensively discussed in Sandi Fox, *For Purpose and Pleasure: Quilting Together in Nineteenth-Century America* (Nashville, Tenn.: Rutledge Hill Press, 1995), pp. 124–26.

5. "The Friend," 1854, Quaker publication, author unknown.

6. Illustrated, with text, in Jennifer Faulds Goldsborough, *Lavish Legacies: Baltimore Album and Related Quilts in the Collection of the Maryland Historical Society* (Baltimore: Maryland Historical Society, 1994), pp. 96–99.

PART 3

"I Botanize and
Read Some, but
Cook a 'Heap'
More"

*F*LOWERS BLOOMED FOR CENTURIES on America's quilts—on printed and painted fabrics, as individual motifs (either pieced or appliquéd), or quilted in tiny stitches—just as they bloomed in America's backyards. Of all that she left behind, the westerning woman must have thought often of her garden. Whether through a slightly formal study of botany or merely the planting of an assortment of seeds and slips, flowers had been the pursuit and the pleasure of these women who now crossed the unfamiliar landscape that lay between them and the Pacific Ocean. All across the miles, they pursued the identification and cataloguing of flowers on the trail, as they had done at home. So it was with Tamsen Donner; in June 1846, as her party traveled near the junction of the North and South Platte Rivers, she wrote:

> We have found the wild tulip, the primrose, the lupine, the ear-drop, the larkspur, and creeping hollyhock, and a beautiful flower resembling the bloom of the beach tree, but in bunches as big as a small sugar-leaf, and of every variety of shade to red and green. I botanize and read some, but cook a "heap" more.[1]

Once the pioneers reached California, the seeds they carried with them would be planted, to flower or not, but the appliquéd quilts they brought were gardens already in full bloom.

NOTE

1. Kenneth L. Holmes, ed., *Covered Wagon Women: Diaries & Letters from the Western Trails: 1840–1890*, vol. 1 (Glendale, Calif. and Spokane, Wash.: The Arthur H. Clark Company, 1983), p. 72.

AMANDA RAND KING'S QUILT

Ohio, ca. 1850
Made by Amanda Rand King
Cotton; appliquéd and quilted
94 x 92 ½ in. (238.8 x 235 cm)
Los Angeles County Museum of Art;
gift of Mrs. Harold Benington

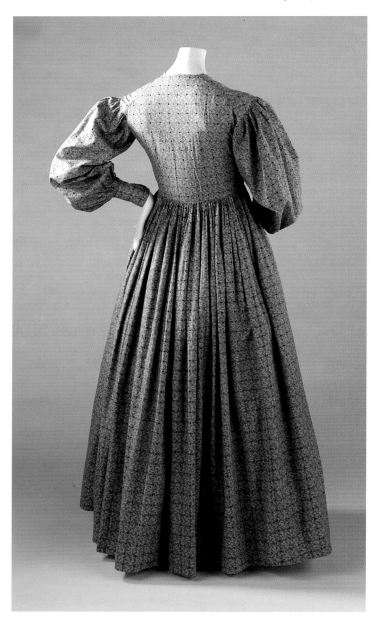

IN CONTRAST TO THE FINE, glazed, relatively expensive furnishing fabrics that were the textiles of choice for *broderie perse* quilts, it was generally the bright cottons of the quiltmaker's day dresses (FIG. 1) that were worked onto the colorful surfaces of America's classic floral appliquéd quilts. Amanda Rand King's stylized botanical motifs (flower, bud, leaf) are deceptively simple, the clear colors she and her children may have worn shown to best advantage on the white ground that was the usual choice. Petaled flowers (centered with a tiny yellow and brown print) were arranged with drooping blossoms, thistles and buds in red, orange, and purple, all growing on leafy, green stems (FIG. 2). The quilt's exuberant central field is separated from its meandering border with a dressmaker's touch: a tiny bit of red piping[1] (FIG. 3). Finally, it was quilted with a design of wreath and plumes and tiny hearts.

Amanda's mid-century flowerpots were worked somewhere in Ohio. The state stood geographically in the path of early western migration, and gradually emigrants from other states joined the New Englanders who had settled there as early as 1788. Quiltmakers had established certain regional traditions and preferences in the places they left behind, and it was in Ohio that many of those merged into new traditions and new preferences. The Ohio quilts that resulted often moved west with daughters and granddaughters, some—like Amanda's—all the way to California.

Amanda Rand King's Quilt

NOTE

1. See the detail of the Sutter's Fort dress, page 23.

FIGURE 2, ABOVE
Amanda Rand King's Quilt (detail)

FIGURE 3, OPPOSITE
Amanda Rand King's Quilt (detail)

[62]

SUSAN BERKELEY'S QUILT

Illinois, ca. 1850
Made by Susan Berkeley's grandmother
Cotton; pieced, appliquéd, embroidered, and quilted
94½ x 86 in. (240 x 218.4 cm)
Los Angeles County Museum of Art; gift of Mrs. Maxine Rucker

THE SPIKED CIRCLES AND SASHING that are the basic elements of this colorful quilt are the same geometric elements of a continuing pattern that is seen on quilts across the United States. Today, when the pattern is referred to by name it is most often called "New York Beauty" or "Road to California," but except for the most classic of patterns, specific names generally appeared later in the nineteenth century than this quilt was made.[1] Although many pattern names grew out of an oral tradition, an almost endless variety of names assigned to an almost endless number of pattern variations[2] came into the twentieth century through professional designers, periodicals, and mail order companies. The names varied regionally and they varied among the printed sources, and their origins continue to be elusive. The early-twentieth-century quilt historian Florence Peto wisely suggested, "It is not wise to be too didactic about the nomenclature of quilt patterns."[3]

Among the women who made quilts and those who admired them, if a quilt was identified by a name, it was more apt to be one associated with the maker or its owner. This is true for *Susan Berkeley's Quilt*, which was made by Susan's grandmother. Family relationships were what mattered, and they mattered most particularly to Susan, because the quilt came to her through the saddest of personal circumstances. Her mother died when Susan was a young child, and her father died a few weeks later; it was determined that Susan and her siblings, now orphans, would be raised separately by various family members. Unfortunately, those family members were distant, one from the other, both geographically and emotionally, and when Susan left her brothers and sisters, she left them forever. As she drove away in a wagon with the aunt and uncle who had assumed responsibility for her upbringing, she was wrapped in this quilt; it had been made for her mother when she was a bride.

The quilt is distinguished by the sixteen flowerpots (FIG. 1) and by the quiltmaker's joyful experimentation with four differing, appliquéd borders. Three of those borders are populated with feeding birds whose wings, beaks, and single eyes are defined by thin, embroidered lines; their heads turn to nibble on the berries that grow from the meandering vines (FIG. 2). This quilt was Susan Berkeley's lone legacy, passed from mother to daughter, California bound.

Susan Berkeley's Quilt

FIGURE 1
Susan Berkeley's Quilt (detail)

NOTES

1. *Godey's Lady's Book* presented three pattern
    names in 1835, but these were descriptive
    rather than fanciful: "hexagon," "six-sided,"
    and "honeycomb patchwork."

2. Barbara Brackman's *Encyclopedia of Pieced
    Quilt Patterns* (Paducah, Ky.: American
    Quilter's Society, 1993) illustrates 4,216
    patterns and variations and often lists sev-
    eral attributable pattern names for each.

3. Florence Peto, *American Quilts and Coverlets:
    A History of a Charming Native Art Together
    with a Manual of Instruction for Beginners*
    (New York: Chanticleer Press, 1949), p. 21.

FIGURE 2
Susan Berkeley's Quilt (detail)

THE "ROSE OF SHARON" QUILT

Monroe County, Missouri, 1857
Made by Margaret and Gillian P. Wright
Cotton; appliquéd, pieced, embroidered, and quilted
96 x 95¾ in. (243.8 x 243.2 cm)
Los Angeles County Museum of Art; gift of Lulu Tyson Russell

THIS SPLENDID QUILT IS THE RESULT of the creative efforts of Margaret and Gillian P. Wright, two sisters in Monroe County, Missouri. Multiple layers of fabric form the complex components of the inventive "Rose of Sharon" variation (FIG. 1) and each of these components is edged in a tiny embroidered chain stitch; bits of soutache form the stems on which the berries hang. Each appliquéd detail is perfect in its selection, placement, and execution; beyond the elaborate swag border, small pieces of folded red fabric form a picot edging containing it all (FIG 2).

FIGURE I
The "Rose of Sharon" Quilt (detail)

The "Rose of Sharon" Quilt

FIGURE 2
The "Rose of Sharon" Quilt (detail)

According to family tradition, this textile was made in celebration of the political victory of the fifteenth president of the United States, James Buchanan (1857–61), and the principal quilting motif is a patriotic triumph—a representation of the American bald eagle as seen on the Great Seal of the United States (FIG 3). In heraldic circles, the eagle would be described as "displayed"—wings and legs fully extended. A shield across his chest, he holds a banderole in his beak with the banner of "Liberty" streaming behind him (at what point did the sisters notice they had misspelled it to read "Libebty"?). The traditional placement in which the talons hold the sheaf of arrows and the olive branch has been reversed, and a drum and drumsticks have been added. Throughout the

FIGURE 3
The "Rose of Sharon" Quilt (detail)

central field and in the border, the quilting has been "stuffed"[1] to further define the pattern, and it is altogether a grand and easily identifiable bird.

The bald eagle was declared our national symbol seventy-five years before the Wright sisters chose it for their quilt, and it appeared in popular profusion over those intervening years. It was worked in all manners of techniques and material: printed and painted, enameled and embroidered, carved and incised and embroidered. Craftsmen had always shared a common vocabulary of design, and the nineteenth-century quiltmaker was included among them.

Remarkably, another quilt was made by these same clever hands. Its elements are of similar design, but each is less fully developed, and the elegant eagles are altogether absent. Time and marriage eventually separated the sisters, and separated the sister-quilts as well; the slightly simpler quilt (was it the first made or the second?) eventually traveled to Texas, while this Missouri masterpiece came west to California.

NOTE

1. Once the quilting design has been outlined in the firmest of quilted stitches, the reverse of the quilt behind each outlined segment is carefully opened by pushing aside a few threads of the fabric. Bits of cotton batting are pushed through the resulting opening to achieve the desired dimension and, finally, the threads are realigned.

SARAH ANN BEEGLE'S QUILT

Baxter Springs, Kansas, ca. 1865
Made by Sarah Ann (Sally) Beegle
Cotton; appliquéd and quilted
94 x 89¾ in. (238.8 x 228 cm)
Los Angeles County Museum of Art; gift of Erma Marsh

FIGURE 1
Sarah Ann Beegle, undated photograph
Collection of Erma Marsh

FIGURE 2
Sarah Ann Beegle's Quilt (detail)

THIS LARGE, APPLIQUÉD QUILT descended through the Beegle family with very little of its history intact. Its attribution to Sarah Ann Beegle would seem to be firm: an oral tradition supported by her photograph (FIG. 1) always tucked away in its folds. "Sally" is thought to have lived in Illinois prior to the Civil War but to have moved at some point to Baxter Springs, Kansas,[1] where, it is assumed, she made her quilt. We are left, then, to consider the object apart from its origins.

The use of a central field surrounded by a running vine border on three sides (FIG. 2) is quite common to the construction of mid-nineteenth-century floral appliqué quilts, but Sarah's quilt is distinctive in the wonderfully graceful manner in which she has arranged a variety of botanical images. On twenty 16-inch appliquéd blocks, slender stems support three stylized roses (sewn with elements of reverse-appliqué) and buds and leaves; each block is then cleverly quarter-turned to form larger motifs of symmetrical sprays.

The rust-brown fabric is probably, and the green possibly, home-dyed. With a very thin batting, the piece is sparsely quilted, but the outline quilting in the border is supplemented with simplistic flowers, leaves, berries, and small hearts, with paired hearts, point-to-point, in the lower corners.

NOTE

1. In 1863, in the midst of the Civil War, William Clark Quantrill and his 450 guerillas swept into Lawrence, Kansas, in the dead of night and, in possibly the greatest atrocity of the war, massacred the men and burned most of the buildings. In October, evading the federal authorities, Quantrill moved across the southeast corner of Kansas toward Texas. Along the way, he attacked the small Federal Post at Baxter Springs; Sarah Beegle may well have been living there during this time. See Alvin M. Joseph Jr., *The Civil War in the American West* (New York: Alfred A. Knopf, 1992), p. 173.

Sarah Ann Beegle's Quilt

THE HUDSON ALBUM QUILT

Possibly Hudson, Michigan, ca. 1880
Quiltmaker unidentified
Cotton; appliquéd and embroidered; inked inscriptions
90¼ x 89¼ in. (229.2 x 226.7)
Natural History Museum of Los Angeles County

WE KNOW LITTLE OF JOHN HUDSON'S LIFE. His 1863 Civil War mustering form listed his occupation as "farmer"; bits of religious ephemera (including a set of scripture cards and an exhorter's license) connect him at some point to a Methodist Episcopal church in Farmersville, Ohio, and various property papers indicate that he (and probably his wife, Lydia) were in Escondido, California, by 1886.[1] This handsome quilt was made for him, but the occasion that inspired the gift is lost to us.

The two blocks done in *broderie perse* echo those found on the most sophisticated pieces from Baltimore, Philadelphia, and New Jersey. The almost-closed wreath of block-printed chintz is outlined in a fine, small, pale-yellow

buttonhole stitch. It is supported by a segment of an arborescent branch from whose tip a fringed flower and leafy plumes dip languidly toward a quilted inscription: "Belle Wade" and the year "1880." It is an intriguing date, stylistically late for both block and quilt. Six other blocks are signed, but except for "S. L. Metzger / Mount Prospect" and "Bill," the other names (inked) are illegible.

Of particular note are two blocks featuring elements of an unidentified fraternal order. Such societies proliferated in the nineteenth century and they developed and shared in a often-secret set of rituals and regalia. These leaf-draped columns (FIG. 1) are probably Masonic references. Following the War of Independence, Masonic symbols became a significant presence in America's decorative arts[2]; by the second half of the nineteenth century, they were seen as single images or primary designs on a number of quilts and bedcovers.[3]

The balance of the motifs is worked primarily in reds and greens, both printed and plain. Standard patterns such as laurel leaves and peonies are coupled with a spectacular assortment of botanical interpretations (FIG. 2). It was particularly skilled hands that applied the two full blocks and the single half-block incorporating the Pennsylvania-German tradition of folded-paper cutting, *scherenschnitte* (FIG. 3). An exceptionally delicate manipulation of the cloth was required to duplicate on quilts the lacy

The Hudson Album Quilt

FIGURE 2
The Hudson Album Quilt (detail)

circles often seen on the paper valentines in that early community. But they do appear with some regularity on the most ambitious of the album quilts worked in Baltimore in the 1840s and 1850s, such as the large (over 9 feet square) quilt assembled by young Sarah Seidenstricker in 1845. A great variety of interlacing circular motifs appeared on a number of its forty-one blocks, each of which is signed in indelible ink.[4] And "It is of interest that the blocks are so placed that they may be read from the top, so that the owner, sitting up in bed, might read the names of her loving friends."[5]

The work of John Hudson's "loving friends" was carefully preserved by his children and grandchildren beyond his own long life, but Sarah Seidenstricker died before she was twenty years old. Her masterwork descended through the family of her husband's second wife.

FIGURE 3
The Hudson Album Quilt (detail)

NOTES

1. The Hudson Papers, The Seaver Center for Western History Research, Natural History Museum of Los Angeles County.

2. Three exemplary exhibition catalogues published by the Scottish Rite Masonic Museum of Our National Heritage in Lexington, Massachusetts, form an important reference for Masonic imagery: *Masonic Symbols in American Decorative Arts* (1976), *Bespangled, Painted & Embroidered: Decorated Masonic Aprons in America 1790–1850* (1980), and *Fraternally Yours: A Decade of Collecting* (1986).

3. More than thirty blocks inspired by the elements of Freemasonry appear on another appliquéd quilt, ca. 1880. Illustrated and discussed in Sandi Fox, *Wrapped in Glory: Figurative Quilts & Bedcovers 1700–1900* (New York and London: Los Angeles County Museum of Art and Thames and Hudson, 1990), pp. 122–27.

4. Sarah Seidenstricker's quilt is illustrated, and each of its forty-one blocks is described in detail, in William Rush Dunton Jr., *Old Quilts* (Catonsville, Md.: published by the author, 1946), pp. 57–62.

5. Dunton, *Old Quilts*, p. 59.

THE "CALIFORNIA ROSE" QUILT

North of San Luis Obispo, California, ca. 1860
Made by Mary Orr Archer
Cotton; appliquéd and quilted
79 x 92 in. (200.7 x 233.7 cm)
Los Angeles County Museum of Art;
gift of Mrs. Wilbur Archer Beckett

IF ADVENTURERS SAW FORTUNES TO BE MADE in the California gold fields, others saw them in collateral commercial activities as well. William Archer had made many trips to California, rounding up wild horses, driving them back to the Missouri River, and selling them to those riding out in search of gold.[1] He had married Virginia-born Mary Orr (born 1828) (FIG. 1) in April 1846, and in 1857 they moved from Des Moines, Iowa, to a ranch north of San Luis Obispo, California. They brought with them a new baby daughter whom they had named Iowa; Mary also brought her considerable quiltmaking skills, and it was there, on Oak Creek, that she worked her California roses (FIG. 2).

The source of the bright reds and green cottons Mary used is unknown, as is the white ground she would later quilt with wreaths and leaves. It could have been purchased from the usually meager selection at a nearby general store, or sent from Iowa by a friend with whom she had quilted in the past, or brought to California with the goods packed in the wagons. In the spring of 1850, for example, Margaret Frink (raised, like Mary Archer, in Virginia on the banks of the Potomac River) prepared to leave her "pleasant and convenient residence" in Indiana to cross the plains:

> The first thing on Mr. Frink's part was to have a suitable wagon made for the trip while I hired a seamstress to make up a full supply of clothing. In addition to our finished articles of dress, I packed a trunk full of dress goods not yet made up.[2]

FIGURE 1
Mary Orr Archer, undated photograph
Collection of Los Angeles County Museum of Art

FIGURE 2, ABOVE
The "California Rose" Quilt (detail)

NOTES

1. Mrs. Wilbur Archer Beckett, letters, April 7, 1975, accession file, Los Angeles County Museum of Art.
2. Kenneth L. Holmes, ed., *Covered Wagon Women: Diaries & Letters from the Western Trails 1840–1890*, vol. 2 (Glendale, Calif. and Spokane, Wash.: The Arthur H. Clark Company, 1983), p. 59.

The "California Rose" Quilt

THE MACHADO QUILT

San Diego, California, ca. 1860
Made by Doña Juana de Dios Machado Alipaz Wrightington
Cotton; appliquéd and quilted
82 x 62½ in. (208.3 x 158.8 cm)
Collection of the San Diego Historical Society;
gift of Everett W. Israel, 1953

IN 1782, DON PEDRO FAGES WAS NEWLY APPOINTED as governor to the Spanish province that included upper and lower California, and he built what would be known as the Governor's Mansion in the center of Monterey. The building was made of local materials (adobe mud bricks, pine, red clay tiles, whitewash from crushed seashells), but with the hope of persuading his much younger wife, Doña Eulalia Fages y de Celis, to leave an elegant *palacio* in Mexico City to travel *El Camino Real* to join him in Monterey, he filled it with elegant objects brought in by the supply ships from San Blas: "a religious image, wall sconces for candles, a gilded mirror, embroidered bed-covers, small rugs, painted Spanish chests to contain his lady's *trousseau*, dishes to rival the Celis', and an elaborate silver service."[1] "Embroidered bed-covers" were in the Spanish tradition; floral appliqué quilts were not.

"I, Juana de Dios Machado, was born in San Diego's old presidio. I do not remember what day, neither the month, nor the year, but I guess I am about sixty-four years of age."[2] It was then 1878, and Juana was being interviewed by Thomas C. Savage, who was acting as an agent for Hubert H. Bancroft. (In an addendum to his work, Savage notes: "Examined the record of baptism. I find she was born in San Diego 8th march 1814."[3]) She was born into one of the oldest families to settle in Alta California. Her father was a corporal in the San Diego Company, and she and her eight siblings were still living in the presidio when the Mexican flag was raised in 1822. Juana remembered this significant political event with one of a more personal nature:

> The next day an order was given to cut the soldiers' braid. . . . Men were used to have braiding and straight hair with a silk ribbon at the ends. Many of their braids arrived to their waists. . . . The order was put to action. I remember when my father arrived to the house with the braid in his hand and handed it to my mother. His face showed sadness and repentance. My mother's face had the same expression while she was looking at the braid and crying.[4]

Juana was married to Damasio Alipas when she was fifteen years old, and she was widowed in 1835 when her husband, a soldier like her father, was killed fighting in Sonora. About 1840 she married Thomas Wrightington, the first American settler in San Diego. A native of Fall River, Massachusetts, a shoemaker by trade, and well educated, Wrightington came to San Diego in 1833 aboard the *Ayucucho* and settled there.[5] Bostonian Richard Henry Dana, in his great personal narrative, *Two Years Before the Mast*, wrote of a day in 1840, when, on liberty with a fellow sailor in San Diego, they

The Machado Quilt

sailor-like, steered for the first grog-shop. This was a small adobe building, of only one room, in which were liquors, "dry-goods," West India goods, shoes, breads, fruits, and everything which is vendible in California. It was kept by a Yankee, a one-eyed man, who belonged formerly to Fall River, came out to the Pacific in a whale-ship, left her at the Sandwich Islands, and came to California and set up a pulperia.[6]

We would not be surprised to hear that Juana de Dios Machado Alipas Wrightington had worked an "embroidered bed-cover"; she recalled in her interview with Mr. Savage that a certain military wife, Doña Lagarda, was skilled in sewing, needlework, and fancywork, and that she and many other girls would go to her house "to learn all her abilities."[7] But the only bedcover attributed to Juana is the cotton, floral appliqué quilt (FIG. 1), with Turkey red *scherenschnitte* double hearts (FIG. 2) surrounded and bordered by leafy stems and vines, all worked on a white, twill weave ground; it is without question in the American tradition.

The quilt is neither signed nor dated[8]; illiterate, Juana left no written record. Attribution is based only on the oral family tradition that accompanied

FIGURE 3
W. P. Blake, *The Mission de Alcala*,
1855, watercolor, size unknown
*Courtesy of the San Diego Historical
Society, Photograph Collection*

the quilt when a descendant presented it to the San Diego Historical Society. But, in fact, in the absence of letters or diaries, notes or photographs, or an inscription on the quilt itself, a family attribution is often the only identifying factor that accompanies a quilt of any origin. A treasured quilt, descended in a family, could have been the work of a long-forgotten maiden aunt once living in the family home, or have been received as the gift of a grateful neighbor.

If the attribution on the *Machado Quilt* receives an uncommon amount of speculation among quilt scholars, it is simply because it is so technically and stylistically contrary to the textiles of Juana Machado's culture. But intermarriage was common in San Diego during that period, and specifically within Juana's immediate family, and when quilts arrived in San Diego (overland or by sea), it is not illogical to think that they could have been part of her visual experience. And once seen, she may well have chosen to work one for herself.

Were an abundance of leafy vines within the quiltmaker's view, or simply recalled in her memory? As seaman Richard Henry Dana rode on from Thomas Wrightington's "grog-shop" to the Mission de Alcala, he observed "the garden, which is a very large one, including several acres filled, it is said, with the best fruits of the climate"[9] (FIG. 3). Earlier, in April 1827, a French navigator, A. Duhaut-Cilly, described the San Diego harbor as the best in all of California, but found little else of merit: "Below the presidio on a sandy plain are seen scattered thirty or forty houses of poor appearance and a few gardens, poorly cultivated."[10]

The quality of those earliest of San Diego's gardens, however, may have been in the observer's eye. A historian has noted that it was the early Spanish soldiers who had planted the first gardens in Old Town; looking down from Presidio Hill they would select a spot "where they could make a comfortable home for their old age and live under their own vine and fig-tree . . ."[11] That comfortable life, under vine and fig-tree, was denied to Juana Machado (FIG. 4), who died an old woman in relative poverty. She was a well-known presence in San Diego where she posed, shortly before her death, in the great cactus hedge in Old Town (FIG. 5).

FIGURE 4
Doña Juana Machado Alipas Wrightington in front of the Wrightington Adobe
in Old Town, San Diego, California,
undated photograph *Courtesy of the San
Diego Historical Society, Photograph
Collection*

FIGURE 5
Doña Juana Machado Alipas
Wrightington in Old Town (detail), San
Diego, California, undated photograph
Courtesy of the San Diego Historical
Society, Photograph Collection

NOTES

1. Susanna Bryant Dakin, *Rose or Rose Thorn?
   Three Women of California* (Berkeley: The
   Friends of the Bancroft Library, University
   of California, 1963), p. 15.
2. Thomas C. Savage, *Los Tiempos Pasados de la
   Alta California: Requerdos de la Sra. Da.
   Juana Machado de Ridington* (sic), 1878.
   MS, the Bancroft Library, University of California, Berkeley.
3. Ibid.
4. Ibid.
5. William E. Smythe, *History of San Diego*,
   vol. 1 (San Diego: The History Company,
   1908), pp. 293–94.
6. Richard Henry Dana Jr., *Two Years Before the
   Mast: A Personal Narrative of Life at Sea*
   (New York: The Heritage Press, 1947),
   p. 102.
7. Savage, *Los Tiempos Pasados*.

8. Previous literature on this quilt has dated it
   as having been made in 1850. In careful
   consultation with the San Diego Historical
   Society, I have redated the piece to ca. 1860.
   If not the earliest quilt made in California, it
   remains an extremely significant artifact.
9. Dana, *Two Years Before the Mast*, p. 105.
10. Quoted in Fr. Zephyrin Engelhardt, *San
    Diego Mission* (San Francisco: James H.
    Barry Co., 1920), p. 216.
11. Smythe, *History of San Diego*, p. 99. "And
    the pioneer of successful gardeners was Cap-
    tain Francisco Maria Ruiz. He planted the
    spot which afterward came to be known as
    Rose's Garden, and his pears, olives and
    pomegranates bore goodly crops for seventy-
    five or eighty years."

PART 4

"Used on the Curly Maple Bed"

*T*HE QUILTS THAT COVERED AMERICA in the first half of the nineteenth century were often bedcoverings of uncommon sophistication: whole cloth quilts of imported pictorial toiles or of glazed wool subtly quilted with immense flowers and plumes; stenciled bedcovers duplicating the decorative motifs found on painted furniture; block- and roller-printed chintz cut apart to form even grander gardens; inventive appliqués and intricately quilted and stuffed whitework. As quiltmakers moved into the second half of the century—and into the western half of the country—sophistication gradually gave way to a sturdiness best exemplified by the pieced quilt; in the closing decades, experimentation with embroidery and embellishment produced surfaces more raucous than refined.

Earlier quilts were often "for best" or "for show," but it was the simple pieced quilt that most often kept Americans warm. The bits of cotton often held tender memories; Lucy Larcom recalled of her New England girlhood that she began her first quilt by collecting a few squares of calico:

> I liked assorting those little figured bits of calico cloth, for they were scraps of gowns I had seen worn, and they reminded me of the persons who wore them. One fragment, in particular, was like a picture to me. It was a delicate pink and brown sea-moss pattern, on a white ground, a piece of a dress belonging to my married sister, who was to me bride and angel in one. I always saw her face before me when I unfolded this scrap—a face with an expression truly heavenly in its loveliness. Heaven claimed her before my childhood was ended. Her beautiful form was laid to rest in mid-ocean, too deep to be pillowed among the soft sea-mosses.[1]

Such, perhaps, were the most significant of the quilts and memories that were carried to California.

NOTE

1. Lucy Larcom, *A New England Girlhood Outlined from Memory* (Boston and New York: Houghton, Mifflin and Company, 1892), pp. 122–23.

THE CHARITY HOPKINS DOLL AND QUILT

Provenance unknown; quilt ca. 1850, doll ca. 1840
Maker unidentified
Cotton; pieced and quilted
25 x 16 in. (63.5 x 40.6 cm)
Natural History Museum of Los Angeles County

FIGURE 1
The Charity Hopkins Doll

FIGURE 2
The Charity Hopkins's Quilt (reverse)

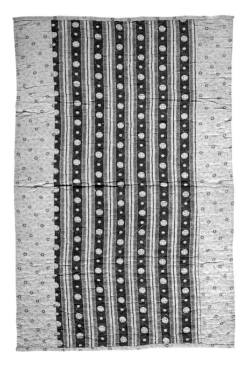

CHARITY HOPKINS STANDS 20 INCHES TALL. Her papier-mâché head—with empire-style hair, molded and painted black, and feathered eyebrows—is turned slightly to the right. Her cloth body features red kid feet and hands, and her costume, in the style of the 1840s, is remarkably detailed and complete. Her woven cotton plaid dress has dropped shoulders and a pointed waist, both appropriate to the period, and ends at the calf. The dress's undersleeves are of dotted Swiss voile, and the elaborate sleeves themselves are fitted with two layers of piped frills. Charity is wearing an elaborate set of undergarments: one plain petticoat, one fancy petticoat with faggoting,[1] a camisole, and sheer ankle-length pantaloons of a complex gauze and twill weave cotton (FIG. 1).

This grandly gowned doll slept in comfortable simplicity, beneath a plain, one-patch, cotton quilt of slightly later date (FIG. 2).

NOTE

1. A lady's cotton petticoat with this detailing, ca. 1830, is illustrated in Margaret Vincent, *The Ladies' Work Table: Domestic Needlework in Nineteenth-Century America* (Allentown, Pa.: Allentown Art Museum, 1988), p. 4. It appears also, near the border, on a quilt of the same period in the collection of the Los Angeles County Museum of Art. As with the piping on *Amanda Rand King's Quilt* (page 61) and on the Sutter's Fort dress (page 22), it is an example of identical sewing techniques applied to both garment and quilt.

The Charity Hopkins Doll and Quilt

THE "BROKEN DISHES" QUILT

Manitou Springs area, Colorado, ca. 1900
Made by Eva Long Stevens
Cotton; pieced and quilted
96 x 95 in. (243.8 x 241.3 cm)
Collection of Cressie Ellen Mendes

FIGURE 1
Eva Long Stevens and her son, Rex
Stevens, in 1903 *Collection of Cressie
Ellen Mendes*

EVA LONG STEVENS'S QUILT WAS A TEXTILE TRIUMPH, both visually and mathematically; based on the "Broken Dishes" pattern, it was constructed from 13,260 pieces of cotton cloth. Worked at the end of the nineteenth century, the quilt slightly preceded one of the great fads of the early twentieth century.

Women had always been quietly competitive regarding their quilts and took pleasure in exhibiting them at fairs and church bazaars; the judgment of their peers was usually based on the design of the quilt and on the size of the pieces and the fineness of the stitch. But by the 1930s, another criteria gained favor—the sheer number of pieces marked and cut and assembled! The *St. Louis-Post Dispatch* reported a Missouri-made quilt of 21,840 pieces, each only ⅝ of an inch square.[1] When Mrs. Jane Long heard of that feat, she went to work, and five months later, on her seventy-eighth birthday, she completed a quilt of 38,000 pieces.[2] Newspapers and periodicals reported such numbers, throwing down a quilted gauntlet. It was in this category of counting that men, who made quilts in far fewer numbers but with equal enthusiasm, seemed to excel. Albert Small, an immigrant to the United States from High Wycombe, England, began with a quilt of 26,141 pieces; his second contained 63,450 and his third a staggering 224,000 minuscule pieces.[3]

It was to Eva's son Rex that this quilt was eventually given; he was nine years old in 1903 when they were photographed together (FIG. 1); Eva was thirty-six. Mr. Stevens wrote a brief biographical essay in which he detailed the early activities of his paternal ancestors. Through five generations, we now know of their service during the Revolutionary War and the Civil War, and of their commercial and academic successes. But of his mother, he wrote only that it was in Meadville, Pennsylvania, that his father, Samuel, "met and married Eva Long who was teaching school there in 1889."[4] But if he did not save for us the small details of his mother's life, he did save—in pristine condition—the ambitious work of her hands (FIGS. 2 and 3).

NOTES

1. Carrie A. Hall and Rose G. Kretsinger, *The Romance of the Patchwork Quilt in America* (Caldwell, Idaho: Caxton Printers, Ltd., 1935), p. 40.
2. Ibid.
3. Janet Carruth and Laurene Sinema, "Emma M. Andres and Her Six Grand Old Characters," *Uncoverings* (1990): 96.
4. Rex Stevens, typescript, n.d.

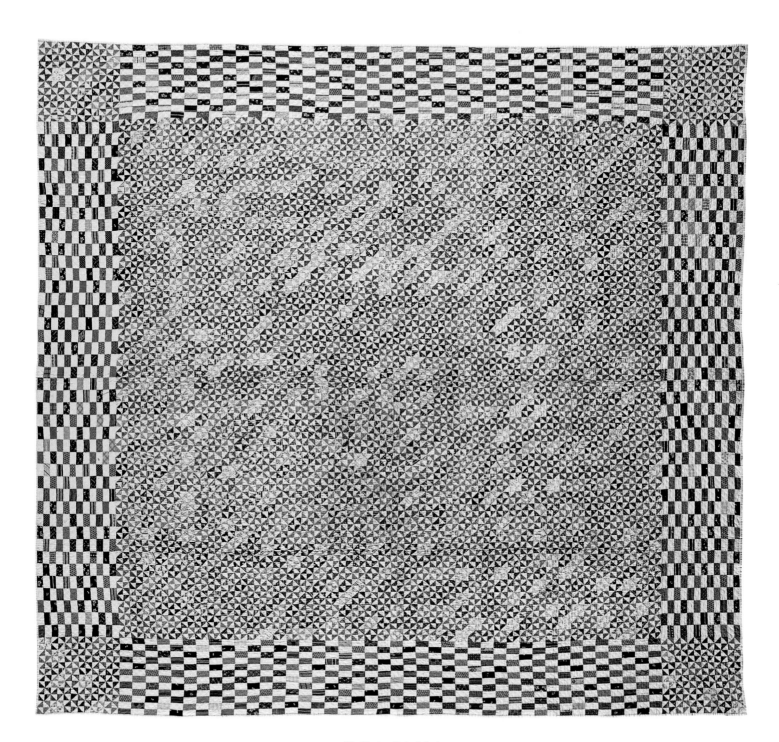

The "Broken Dishes" Quilt

FIGURE 2, OPPOSITE
The "Broken Dishes" Quilt (detail)

FIGURE 3, ABOVE
The "Broken Dishes" Quilt (detail)

THE HAYES FAMILY QUILTS

"ZIGZAG"

Farmington, New Hampshire, ca. 1853
Made by Lydia Hayes
Cotton; pieced and quilted
86 x 85 in. (218.4 x 215.9 cm)
Riverside Municipal Museum

"CROSSED SASHING"

Farmington, New Hampshire, ca. 1860
Made by a member of the Hayes family
Cotton; pieced and quilted
114 x 116 in. (289.6 x 294.6 cm)
Riverside Municipal Museum

THERE WAS A TRADITION OF QUILT OWNERSHIP in the Hayes family; in a handwritten, nineteenth-century New Hampshire inventory,[1] several were listed under "Household Furniture" along with beds, underbeds, bed cords, and feather beds:

1 blue bedquilt	6.00
1 cotton and wool coverlet	4.00
4 calico quilts	3.00
2 small calico quilts	.75
2 bed comfortables	2.00
1 old do [ditto]	.50
1 French calico quilt	1.00
1 fancy counterpane	7.50

There was a tradition of quiltmaking as well. In Farmington, New Hampshire, the dry goods store owned by Simon French Hayes provided an abundance of cotton fabrics for his wife, Lydia (1808–1882) and his daughters Lydia (1833–1861), Phebe (1835–1917), and Mary Ann (1845–1919). A granddaughter, Katie, born in 1866, the year her grandfather died, would eventually join that family circle of quilters. It was Katie who eventually kept the results of their labors together as a body of work numbering over twenty pieced quilts and comforters.

The family often wintered in the San Bernardino Mountains outside of Riverside, California, eventually moving to the area in 1903; notes attached to several of the quilts in the repository indicate that several of them were pieced during those pleasant times. Other notes connect the objects to their history:

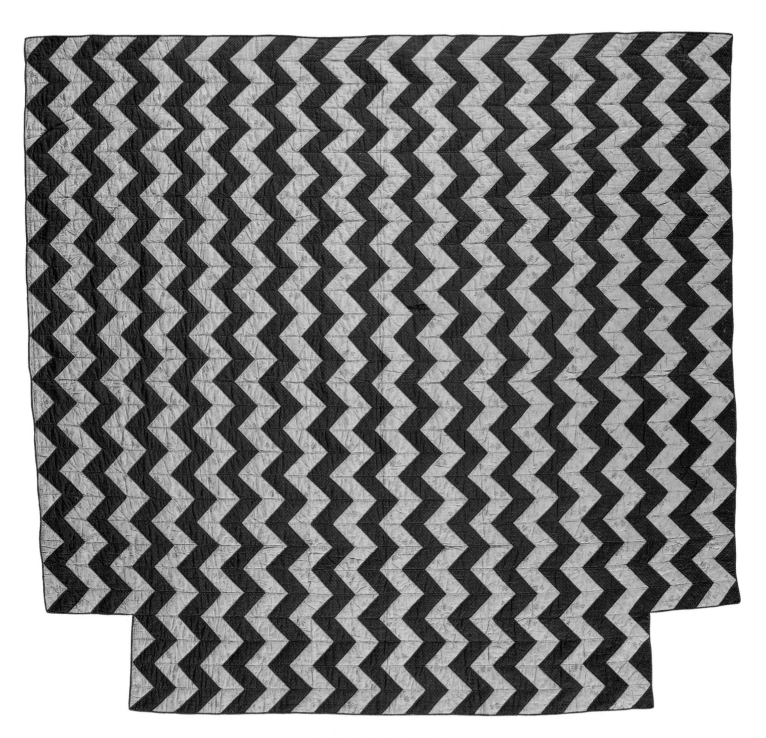

The Hayes Family Quilts, "ZigZag"

Aunt Lydia's French Patch comforter made about 1853 when engaged to Henry Jenkins. She did not marry him. [Lydia married Orin Tenny Fall, and when she died, at age twenty-eight, Orin married her youngest sister, Mary Ann.]

Comforter with red stripes. Henry liked it as Mother gave it to him and it has been on his bed ever since.

Grandmother's Irish Patchwork. Aunt Phebe said the brown striped, figured pieces were French patch bought by Grandfather at .50 a yard.

The *Hayes Family Quilts* (FIGS. 1 and 2) were surely made for two four-posted beds that feature prominently in the family's material memories:

[The bed] was made from a Curley Maple tree from the old "wood lot" near the Black House (unpainted) where Grandma Phebe was born. There was also a dresser made from the same tree and a second bed set made from a Birdseye Maple from the same "wood Lot." Both bed sets were made at the same time—one for Phebe and one for Lydia Hayes, about 1850 or earlier, ordered by their father Simon French Hayes . . .[2]

A third similarly shaped quilt of a very large, dark blue-figured wool was made by Lydia at "Black House":

The delaine cloth of which it is made grandfather & grandmother got on a trip to Concord where they went with team on business. It was used on the curly maple bed.

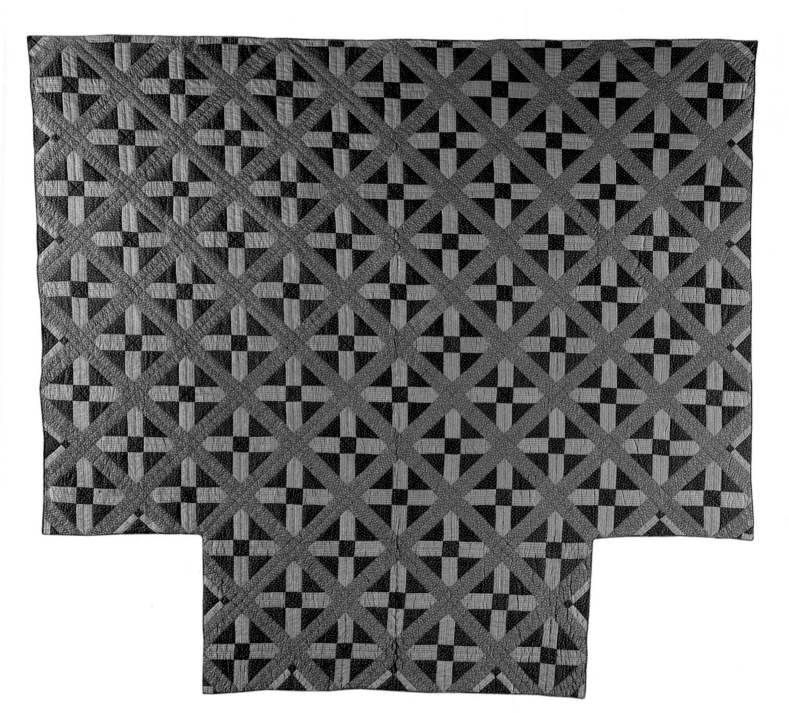

The Hayes Family Quilts, "Crossed Sashing"

Pieces of very old comforter.

Pieces of very old worn out comforter.

FIGURE 3
"Pieces of very old comforter" *Hayes repository, Riverside Municipal Museum*

FIGURE 4
"Pieces of very old worn out comforter" *Hayes repository, Riverside Municipal Museum*

Integral to the quilts, there has descended with them an extensive collection of small fabric samples, neatly attached to inexpensive sheets of paper. Two pages hold pieces of a very old worn-out comforter (FIGS. 3 and 4), but several hold pieces of cotton fabrics that can be matched to fabrics used in the quilts, particularly in the case of a comforter on which is embroidered "Katie aged 6 yrs."

Most of the other pages continue a centuries-old tradition in which a woman collected small pieces of fabric that were precious and personal to her. These were usually affixed to a piece of paper, annotated with descriptions of the pieces of clothing for which they had been used; the date, source, and cost were occasionally included as well. The most significant example of this charming pastime is the collection of silks, wools, and cottons assembled in England between 1746 and 1823 by Barbara Johnson, the daughter of a well-to-do cleric.[3] At some point, she pinned her souvenirs onto the pages of a large, bound account book that had been used by a young professional man, George Thomson, between 1738 and 1748.[4] The opening page is breathtaking! The bits of richly colored fabric remain bright, and her handwriting is firm and clear:

a flower'd Calicoe long sack 1746

a Blue damask Coat 1746 / half a Guinea a yard

a flower'd Cotton jacket 1747

a blue & white linnen long sack / 1748

a flower'd silk Robe-Coat 1748

Almost two centuries later, many unbound pages in the Hayes repository (FIG. 5) were similarly inspired.[5]

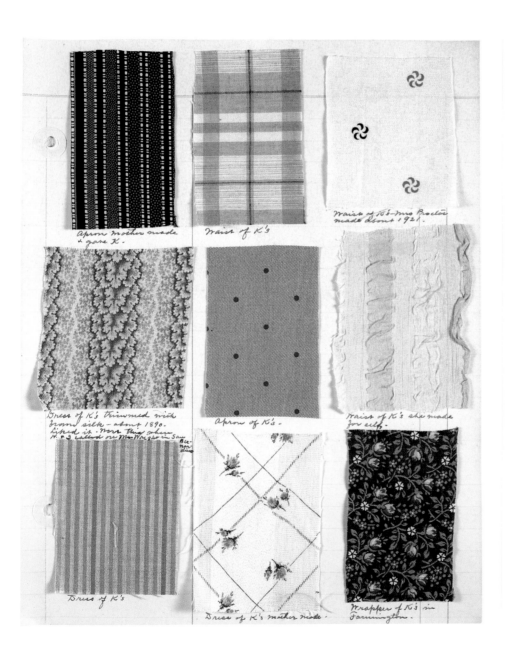

FIGURE 5
Annotated fabric patches *Hayes repository, Riverside Municipal Museum*

NOTES

1. Hayes Family Papers, Riverside Municipal Museum.
2. Object Report, Riverside Municipal Museum.
3. Barbara Johnson's Album was researched and conserved at the Victoria & Albert Museum in London; it is meticulously reproduced in Natalie Rothstein, ed., *A Lady of Fashion: Barbara Johnson's Album of Styles and Fabrics* (London: Thames and Hudson, 1987).
4. Large portions of Thomson's entries are visible, providing a second scholarly resource in his description of his expenses. In addition to the expenses associated with lodging and dining, travel and servants, his purchases included a great deal of fashionable clothing, books, and chocolate, "Two tickets for the Ball Haymarkett," "Pictures bought at the Apollo Coffee House," "Lost at cards."
5. The patches read: "Apron Mother made / + gave K.," "Waist of K's," "Waist of K's— Mrs. Proctor / made about 1921," "Dress of K's trimmed with / brown silk—about 1890 / liked it—wore this when / H (+) I called on Mrs. Wright in San / Ber / nar / dino," "Apron of K's," "Waist of K's she made / for self," "Dress of K's," "Dress of K's Mother made," "Wrapper of K's in / Farmington."

THE "GOD AND GRANT" QUILT

Unionville, California, ca. 1878
Made by Susan Deering Lohry
Cotton; pieced and quilted, painted
80 x 62 in. (203.2 x 157.5 cm)
Marshall Gold Discovery State Historic Park

SUSAN LOHRY (1824–1884) AND HER HUSBAND, Adam, moved from Kentucky to Missouri in 1846, and in 1853 they left that jumping-off state for California in a covered wagon with a baby, four young children all under the age of eight, and great expectations. Instead, as for many, California held disaster ("Their brick home, built ... in 1858, was burned to the ground when a four-year-old child, carrying a candle, accidentally set the curtains on fire"[1]), disappointment (Adam's handwritten notes in the family Bible include the "... mention of an older daughter's elopement [her name is outlined in black])," and the death of three of their ten children (two died as infants, a son at age nineteen). And it brought to Susan an unspeakable tragedy:

> In 1880, Adam committed suicide by drowning himself in the American River, which ran through the back of their property. He was distraught over the theft of gold left in the safe of his [general] store for safekeeping by local miners. His son-in-law was convicted and sent to state prison for the crime....
>
> Susan placed an ad in the Placerville *Mountain Democrat*, offering a fifty-dollar reward for the recovery of Adam's body. The ad ran for one month, but no follow-up article indicates any recovery. A family burial plot in the Lotus cemetery, however, contains a tall marker with Adam's name engraved on it.[2]

Susan's grave is unmarked. She is remembered instead by this surprising quilt: one would scarcely expect to turn over a pieced quilt and find a large presidential campaign banner on its reverse! (FIG. 1)

From the beginning, America's political history was written on a variety of textiles and those textiles were often incorporated into America's quilts. In 1776, in England, engravings celebrating the heroes of our independence were translated onto copperplate-printed textiles; one of the most popular presented the *Apotheosis of Franklin and Washington* complete with allegorical figures, leopard-drawn chariots, and banners proclaiming "Where Liberty Dwells, There is My Country." These furnishing fabrics often were worked into imposing whole-cloth quilts.

The political campaigns of the next century saw the production of endless political promotion in a variety of printed textiles that also found their way into quilts and bedcovers.[3] Portraits of the candidates or of their campaign symbols spread across a sea of yardage from which squares, rectangles, and triangles were snipped and pieced into quilt tops; groups of bright bandanas formed the central field of children's quilts and comforters; and silk campaign ribbons were carefully saved to embellish the surfaces of silk and velvet crazy quilts.

The "God and Grant" Quilt

NOTES

1. All the facts used in this entry regarding Susan Lohry's life are the result of careful research done by members of the California Heritage Quilt Project. I am indebted to them for their fine work, and I am grateful to Jean Ray Laury for permission to recount it here; see Jean Ray Laury and the California Heritage Quilt Project, *Ho for California! Pioneer Women and Their Quilts* (New York: E. P. Dutton, 1990), pp. 67–69.

2. Ibid.

3. Herbert Ridgeway Collins, *Threads of History: America Recorded on Cloth 1775 to the Present* (Washington, D.C.: Smithsonian Institution Press, 1979).

4. Roger Butterfield, *America's Past* (New York: Simon and Schuster, 1976), p. 197.

By 1868, Ulysses S. Grant and the "Union Victories" had moved great masses of Union veterans into the ranks of Republican voters; the "Boys in Blue" arrived from all over the North to march, in uniforms, in support of the presidential campaign of their former commander. The torchlight parade held in Philadelphia on October 2, 1868, was a political extravaganza of the highest order. Bunting was draped, flags were flown, cornet bands played, fireworks exploded overhead, and banners were held high over the throng while thousands of handheld torches illuminated the entire event. It is interesting to suppose what Grant might have thought about this event, and all the other torchlight events that followed, because he was known to dislike politics and political talk, military parades, and martial music.[4]

It is difficult to know where this campaign banner originated. It is hand-painted and might not have been included in a highly organized, cosmopolitan parade; it would have been an important addition to a slightly more modest event. If not of California origin, a sturdy piece of fabric such as this would have been a valued addition to the outfit of a traveler moving west by wagon.

It is easier to identify the origin of the variety of predominantly brown and pink printed cottons that comprise the pieced top of this quilt (FIG. 2); they were probably leftovers from the construction of dresses for Susan Deering Lohry and her daughters, three of whom helped her make the quilt.

FIGURE 2
The "God and Grant" Quilt (detail)

THE SOLDIER'S QUILT

Provenance unknown, ca. 1901
Quiltmaker unidentified
Cotton and silk; pieced, appliquéd, and embroidered
79 x 69¼ in. (200.7 x 175.9 cm)
Collection of Mike Reinoso

REMARKABLE CIRCUMSTANCES SURELY SURROUNDED the construction of this utterly fascinating quilt, but as yet research has revealed only that it was made by a soldier recovering from injuries received in the Spanish American War and came to California through marriage into a family descended from John Sutter.

The custom of a wounded warrior wielding a needle during the idle hours of his convalescence was a particularly British tradition during the second half of the nineteenth century. English soldiers' quilts (primarily associated with their service in India and with the Crimean War, which began in 1854) were constructed of small patches of uniform fabric pieced into strong geometric patterns.[1] Prior to the introduction of khaki, regimental uniforms presented a colorful palette with gray, navy, or black jackets and trousers faced with a variety of greens, blues, purples, scarlets, and yellows; vermillion, turquoise, salmon, and orange were colors particular to their uniforms in India. In a variety of wools, the small textile fragments came from the tailoring or alteration of uniforms, or from the uniforms of those that had fallen in battle. This American soldier's quilt was worked in similarly vibrant colors, twentieth-century cottons

pieced into a brilliant star of Bethlehem. It was in 1898, during the McKinley administration, that its maker had fought in what John Hay, the American ambassador in London, viewed as "a splendid little war."[2]

Photographs of four American presidents have been pasted onto the star's surface: Lincoln, Grant (FIG. 1), Garfield (FIG. 2), and McKinley (all but Grant were assassinated: Lincoln in 1865, Garfield in 1881, and McKinley in 1901). The photographs of Lincoln, Grant, and Garfield were produced in a cluster; the images were based on photographic engravings such as those one might have found in *Harper's Weekly*. Steel engravings were made directly from a photograph and printed in an unidentified popular magazine. Some entrepreneur took a photograph of each printed image. These were then commercially mass-produced, mounted on cardboard, and sold as political mementos. The

The Soldier's Quilt

FIGURE 2
The Soldier's Quilt (detail)

photographs are in themselves a technically interesting study: those of Lincoln, Grant, and Garfield were taken in natural light, that of McKinley under then-available studio lights (indicated by the light bouncing off his forehead and the back of his head). The lithograph of Grant was heavily retouched, that of Garfield more artfully so. All four are silver gelatin prints; McKinley's has a warmer sepia tone and the others possibly a selenium tone, giving them their purplish hue.[3]

Small woven American flags encircle the central field and a few silk flags of foreign nations (possibly tobacco premiums) are included on the quilt. But most intriguing are the odd shapes that surround the star[4] (FIGS. 3 and 4). Now identified, they are handmade, silk duplicates of Civil War corps badges, held fast to the yellow sateen ground with embroidered featherstitches. The use of corps badges purportedly was inspired by an incident in June 1862, in which Union General Philip Kearney, having mistakenly chastised members of a division not under his command, directed his officers to sew identifying 2-inch pieces of red flannel to the tops of their caps; the enlisted men in his division soon followed suit, cutting and wearing their own red badges. On March 21, 1863, on orders from Major General Joseph Hooker, corps badges were adopted for all units of the Army of the Potomac and by the time the war ended, they had been adopted by all but two of the Union Army Corps. To identify each badge on this soldier's quilt— by its shape and by the small silk number sewn to its surface—is to read the story of that terrible war.

NOTES

1. For attribution, the Royal Army Museum in London requires that the quilts be constructed from "genuine military fabric described by dress regulations and sewn by military personnel"; see Janet Rae et al., *Quilt Treasures of Great Britain* (Nashville, Tenn.: Rutledge Hill Press, 1996), p. 171.

2. John Hay to Theodore Roosevelt, quoted in Roger Butterfield, *The American Past* (New York: Simon and Schuster, 1976), p. 282.

3. Dr. Jonathan Spaulding, Associate Curator and head of the Seaver Center for Western History Research at the Natural History Museum of Los Angeles County, very generously provided these observations on the photographs.

4. The excitement of discovering and interpreting this unique historical artifact has been shared with Dr. Tom Sitton, Curator of History, and Beth Werling, Collections Manager, at the Natural History Museum of Los Angeles County. I am exceedingly grateful to them for their invaluable research assistance, and to Dorothy Ettensohn, who brought the *Soldier's Quilt* to our attention.

FIGURE 3
The Soldier's Quilt (detail)

FIGURE 4
The Soldier's Quilt (detail)

ANNA HALL'S QUILT

Rogers Mesa, Colorado, marked 1903
Made by Mrs. Anna Elizabeth Cumpton Hall
Wool, cotton, velvet, silk, and flannel; pressed and embroidered
82 ½ x 63 ½ in. (209.6 x 161.3 cm)
Collection of Herb Wallerstein

CARVED ON STONE IN QUIET CEMETERIES and written and recorded in county courthouses, the major records of a family's past—births and marriages and deaths—were, of necessity, left behind by the western traveler. Some few could be carried in a crowded wagon (those on a tenderly folded marriage certificate or on the fragile pages of a thick family Bible), but for the most part, the recording of rites of passage would have to begin anew. Many were written down during the journey west, in cramped script in journals and diaries, and these would suffice until the emigrants had reached a more permanent place and established new cemeteries, new courthouses.

Anna Elizabeth Hall (1834–1906) must have drawn on all the records she could gather, or remember, to construct this extravagantly detailed family register. She had married Daniel Chapfield Hall on December 9, 1849, in Madison, Jefferson County, Illinois, when she was a girl of fifteen. Anna and Daniel had eleven children; all, with the possible exception of the last, Laura Catherine, had been born in Keokuk County, Iowa. Little Laura died in Benton County, Missouri, before her first birthday; Daniel died a few weeks earlier on July 6, 1871, at forty-five years of age. Anna had lost other children: David Clement, her first-born, at four years of age, and Charles Sherman, her eighth, at less than three months. These were to be Anna's years of sorrow. Her tenth child, Grace Jane, would also die young, at twenty-one; Martha, just married, died in childbirth in Missouri.[1]

FIGURE I
Anna Hall's Quilt (detail)

Anna worked a quilt block for each of her children. In the neatest of cross-stitches she entered their name, their spouse's name and the date of their marriage, their children's names, and birth dates for all. And for four of those dear children now lost to her—Laura, David, Charles, and Grace Jane (FIG. 1)—the date of their deaths. There were twelve blocks in all, including one for herself and Daniel: Charles Sherman Hall, Laura Catherine Hall, David Clement Hall, Daniel Edgar Hall, Grace Jane Hall, John Moses Hall, Stephen Divine Hall, Father

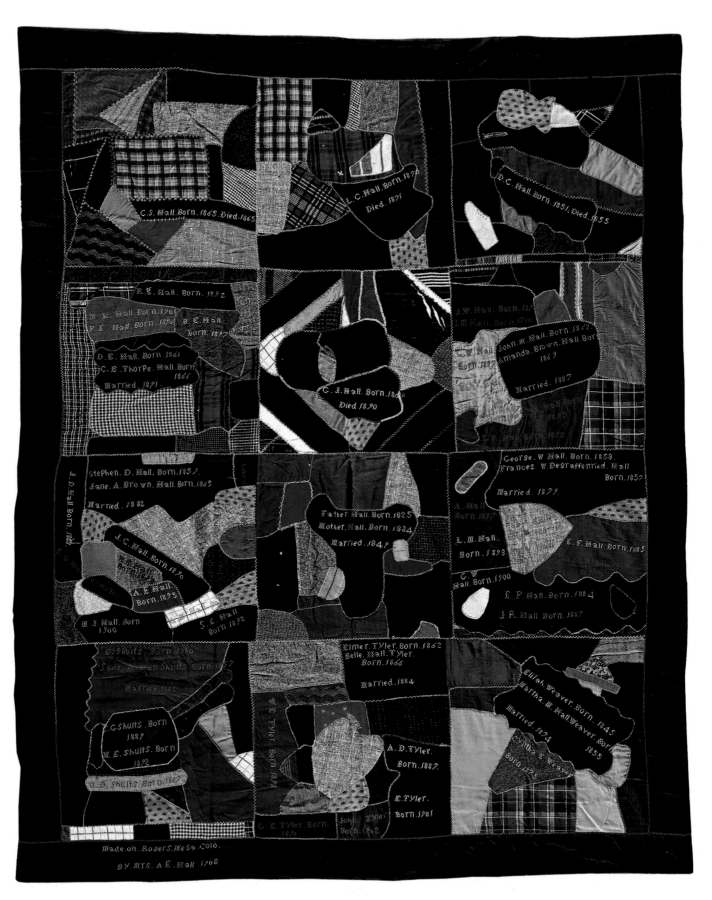

Anna Hall's Quilt

FIGURE 2
Anna Hall's Quilt (detail)

Hall / Mother Hall, George Washington Hall (FIG. 2), Sarah (Sadie) Amanda Hall, Belle (Anna) Hall, Martha Mariah Hall.

This style of quilt—a crazy quilt, primarily in wools and cottons, with multiple embroidered names and/or initials—was particularly popular around the turn of the century. In stark contrast to Anna's tidy cross-stitched entries, the names on the others often were entered in script in rather thick wool yarn. The surface of one such quilt, worked by Edith Withers Meyers on her family's homestead in the Nebraska panhandle, is additionally rich with notes of intriguing social activities: "Promenade / dancing on the / bridge," "Swede Dance," and "Skating Party on / North River." This was the quilted souvenir of a young woman: Edith was eighteen years old when she began her quilted diary and twenty-two when she inscribed "12 1898 / done at last."[2] Anna was almost seventy years old when she worked her final, tidy, multicolored cross-stitches: "Made.On.Rogers. Mesa.Colo. / By.Mrs. A.E.Hall.1903" (FIG. 3).

Born and married in Illinois, bearing children in Iowa, and widowed in
Missouri, Anna (with many of her grown children) seems next to have moved
to Colorado. Her journeys west were soon completed: by 1905 almost all of
the Hall family were living in Southern California; it was there, a year later, in
Ontario, San Bernardino County, that Anna died.

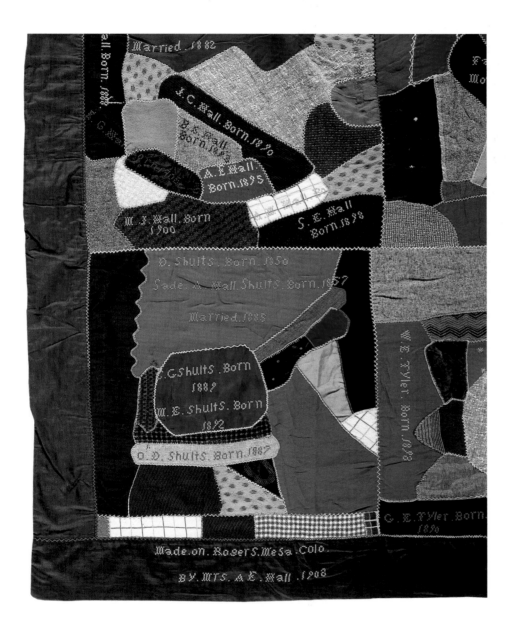

FIGURE 3
Anna Hall's Quilt (detail)

NOTES

1. The Hall family genealogy was assembled
   by Jean Wheeler, Anna and Daniel Hall's
   great-granddaughter.
2. Illustrated in Patricia Cox Crews and
   Ronald C. Naugle, eds., *Nebraska Quilts and
   Quiltmakers* (Lincoln and London: University of Nebraska Press, 1991), p. 155.

THE BIDWELL MANSION'S WOOL QUILT

Probably Butte County, California, ca. 1900
Maker unidentified
Wool and cotton; pieced and embroidered
63 x 52 ³⁄₁₆ in. (160 x 132.5 cm)
California State Parks, Bidwell Mansion State Historic Park

FIGURE 1
The Bidwell Mansion's Wool Quilt
(detail)

JOHN BIDWELL WAS AMONG THE PRINCIPAL ORGANIZERS and leaders of the 1841 Bartleson Party, that first over-land attempt by wagons to cross the Sierra Nevada Mountains into Alta California. The wagons would have to be abandoned, but the ragged pioneers eventually rode and walked into the San Joaquin Valley. Having survived extraor-dinary hardships, Bidwell began almost at once to secure for himself great wealth and political prominence, and by 1849 he initiated the purchase of the Rancho del Arroyo Chico, 26,000 acres of fertile land in the Sacramento Valley on which he would make his fortune and his reputation as one of California's leading agricultur-alists.[1] It was here that he eventually built the grand three-story Italian-style country villa that houses this embroidered and be-ruffled wool quilt.

A half-century earlier, more plainly presented, wool was the cloth in which many women traveled to California:

> A suitable dress for prairie traveling is of great import to health and comfort. Cot-ton or linen fabrics do not sufficiently protect the body against the direct rays of the sun at midday, nor against rays or sudden changes of temperature. Wool, being a nonconductor, is the best material for this mode of locomotion, and should always be adopted for the plains.[2]

Cloth for clothing was also cloth for quilts. The curved elements in this pieced quilt (FIG. 1) were cut from a variety of sources and times, from new cloth and recycled portions of less-worn, discarded clothing, much of it difficult to date because of the relative plainness of the fabric. There in the home of one of California's earliest pioneers, sentiment might wish us to identify one of those bits of wool as having come from a trail dress, but few of those survived the rigors of travel and terrain; occasionally a small, deteriorated scrap was cut to save as a relic, affixed to a small scrap of paper identifying it as a reminder of that great journey.

This pattern is classic, and it was extensively worked in cotton and wool both here and in England for over a century.[3] In San Francisco, in February

The Bidwell Mansion's Wool Quilt

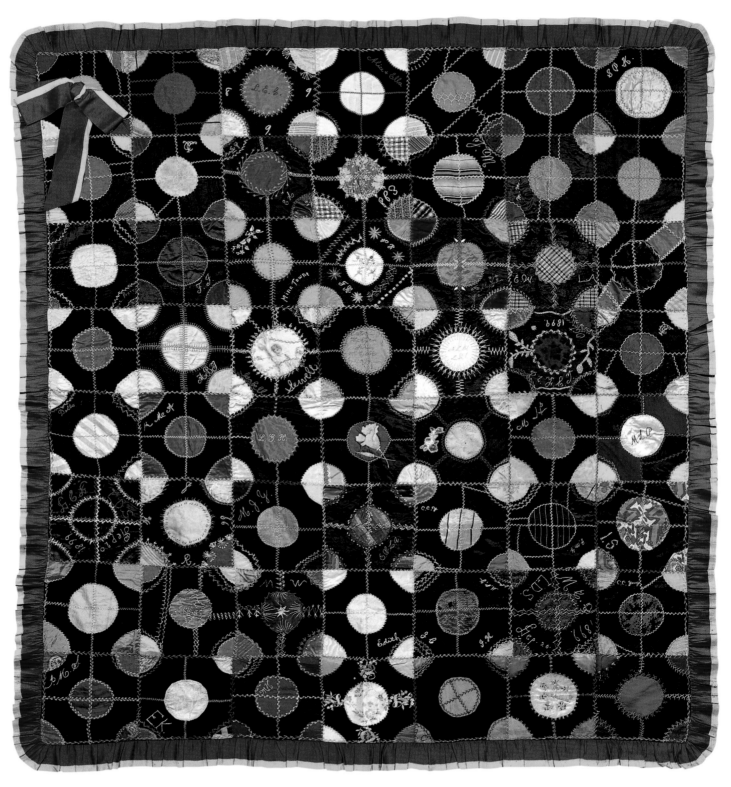

FIGURE 2
Sister Hattie Nye's Quilt, San Francisco,
California, 1900, 68 x 61 in. (172.7 x
154.9 cm) *Courtesy of Museum of Church
History and Art, Salt Lake City*

1900, the principal decorative elements of the Butte County quilt were duplicated on a silk quilt (FIG. 2), but each element was technically and aesthetically enhanced. The simple featherstitch worked over each seam line was joined by a variety of others—herringbone, chain, and French knots for example—in polychrome silk threads. The surface was further embellished by a variety of names and initials and by figurative and floral designs; a silk bow echoed the striped ruffle. The quilt was worked by the members of a local Women's Relief Society of the Church of Latter-Day Saints and given to Harriet (Hattie) Horspool Nye as " . . . a loving 'souvenir' of your sojourn in the Golden State of California amongst us, and which may last long after we are laid to our eternal rest"[4] (FIG. 3).

FIGURE 3
Sister Hattie Nye's Quilt (detail)

NOTES

1. Linda Rawlings, ed., *Dear General: The Private Letters of Annie E. Kennedy and John Bidwell 1866–1868* (Sacramento: California Department of Parks and Recreation, 1993).

2. Captain Randolph B. Marcy, *The Prairie Traveler: A Hand-book for Overland Expeditions* (Washington, D.C.: War Department, 1859), p. 37. Appropriate clothing was critical to the journey, and although it was assumed that women would have mending materials with them, *The Prairie Traveler* (p. 39) reminded each man to have in his outfit "Stout linen thread, large needles, a bit of beeswax, a few buttons, paper of pins, and a thimble, all contained in a small buckskin or stout cloth bag."

3. On a quilt made for "John and Elizabeth Chapman" in 1820, the pattern is worked in early printed cottons and surrounds a central-medallion panel commemorating the Duke of Wellington (Collection of the Victoria & Albert Museum, London).

4. For additional text on Sister Hattie Nye's quilt, see Sandi Fox, *For Purpose and Pleasure: Quilting Together in Nineteenth-Century America* (Nashville, Tenn.: Rutledge Hill Press, 1995), pp. 156–59.

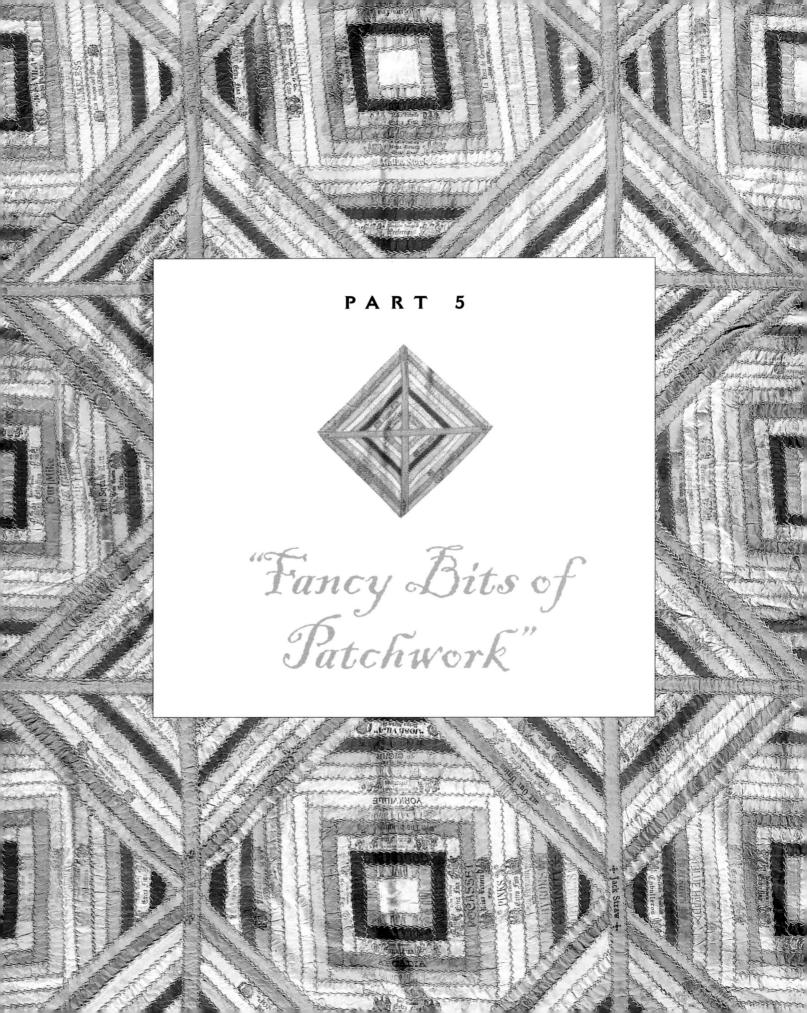

PART 5

"Fancy Bits of Patchwork"

*I*N THE LAST QUARTER OF THE NINETEENTH century, the graceful, flowing curves of floral appliqué and the logical geometric organization of pieced quilts were the principal components of the quiltmaker's repertoire. But a new quilt was soon in the making, an asymmetrical extravaganza of silks and satins, velvets and brocades, and—somewhat later—richly colored wools. The enthusiastic embellishment of these "crazed" surfaces, with all manners of embroidery and ribbons, beads and spangles, resulted in surfaces considered either opulent or overwrought, according to one's aesthetic taste.

The beginnings of this new genre coincided with the nation's celebration of its own beginnings a hundred years past. In 1866, with the Civil War recently ended and the nation whole once again, it was suggested[1] that plans should be laid for a grand celebration, ten years hence, to mark the hundredth anniversary of the signing of the Declaration of Independence. The Centennial Exposition in Philadelphia[2] opened on May 10, 1876, on 450 acres in Fairmount Park, across the Schuylkill River.

A confluence of factors led to the creation of crazy quilts (England's Royal School of Art Needlework, for example, certainly provided the technical challenge), but it was the Japanese presence at the exposition that was primary. Japanese paintings had entered the European market in the 1850s and had influenced painters such as James Abbott McNeill Whistler in the early 1860s. But the asymmetrical aspects of *Japonisme* did not become an influence on American quilts until the immense popular response to Japan's pavilion and its contents had created a wave of enthusiasm for all things Japanese. In 1885, *Harper's Bazar* continued to proclaim that "Japanese confusion, which is at heart the highest artistic order, reigns."[3]

NOTES

1. That suggestion seems first to have come in from John L. Campbell, an Indiana college professor, in letters to his senator and to the mayor of Philadelphia. See Lynwood Mark Rhodes, "Uncle Sam's 100th Birthday Party—1876," *The American Legion Magazine* (February 1973): 21.
2. The official name was "The International Exhibition of Arts, Manufactures, and Products of the Soil and Mine."
3. *Harper's Bazar*, July 25, 1885, p. 475.

THE FLORAL CRAZY QUILT

Chicago, Illinois, ca. 1885
Quiltmaker unidentified
Silk, satin and velvet; pressed, embroidered, and embellished
82 ½ x 65 ¾ in. (209.6 x 167 cm)
Natural History Museum of Los Angeles County

IN BOTH THEIR COSTUMES AND CUSTOMS, American colonists had always sought to reflect that which was fashionable in England, and even after their hard-won independence, that sense of reliance remained intact; the advice they sought arrived in a timely fashion by letters and ladies' magazines. A hundred years later, those same means were used by women in the West to keep abreast of fashionable dress and activities in the East. In 1885, for only ten cents, an ambitious quiltmaker in even the most remote California town could acquire details on how to master the complexities of the crazy quilts that were worked in the most fashionable of eastern parlors. In his small but comprehensive booklet, *Ornamental Stitches for Embroidery* (FIG. 1), T. E. Parker of Lynn, Massachusetts, was pleased to provide "Instructions for Making Crazy Patchwork":

> Crazy Patchwork has now become so popular as to require but little instruction. As the name indicates, it is simply sewing together odd bits of Silk, Satin, Plush, etc. in a "haphazard" sort of way, so that the angles may somewhat imitate the craze or crackle of old china, from which all this kind of work derives its name. The ornamenting of the seams with fancy stitches in bright-colored silks gives very pleasing effect . . .[1]

FIGURE 1

Ornamental Stitches for Embroidery, folios
Collection of Kay Cynova

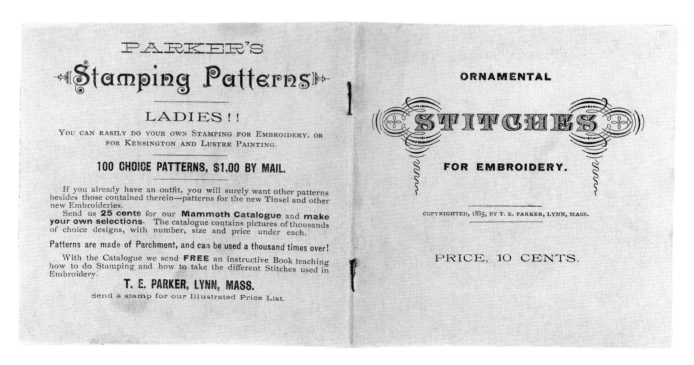

The Floral Crazy Quilt

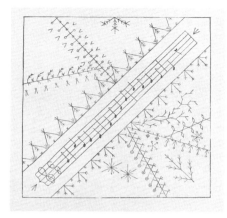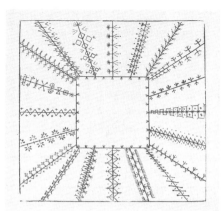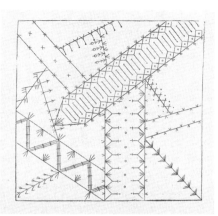

In text and illustrations, the booklet detailed the varieties of embroidery stitches that were appropriate as embellishment (outline, Kensington, plush or tufted stitch, arrasene, and chenille), and the manner in which they could be overlaid and combined (FIG. 2). In addition to the embellishment of the seams, a number of motifs and objects floated crazily across the quilt. Among those embroidered elements, things Japanese were especially favored (the cranes that

FIGURE 4
The Floral Crazy Quilt (detail)

stood in the gardens of the pavilion in the exposition, fans, owls, tiny insects, and silk souvenir ribbons from political parties, fraternal orders, and firemen's conventions were sought-after additions.

But the maker of a crazy quilt that would eventually travel from Chicago to California with the Arms family was focused almost solely on flowers (FIG. 3). Between the intricately embellished seams, individual blossoms and small sprays were planted colorfully on every flat surface, and four larger sprays adorned the middle of each border. The piece is particularly grand in the quilt-maker's extensive use of satin carefully folded into an abundance of dimensional roses and buds (FIG. 4). As was frequently the case, the quiltmaker chose to back the piece with a maroon silk, commercially quilted (FIG. 5). This singular subject was not surprising, for the fascination with botanical images that was manifested in those mid-century floral appliqués continued unabated. And a few years earlier, in 1882, an additional influencing element had arrived in America in the form of Oscar Wilde. This distinguished but controversial representative of England's Aesthetic art movement toured the United States for a series of lectures, and at each stop almost every journalist addressed his aesthetic approach to fashion and flowers. In Boston, he was seen

> wearing a light-brown velvet coat, a waistcoat of yellowish silk, blue tie and stock-ings, low brown shoes, and lemon-colored gloves. The hat was large and of a dif-ferent shade of brown, and from under it the straight hair reached almost to the shoulder.[2]

FIGURE 5
The Floral Crazy Quilt (detail)

FIGURE 6
Ye Soul and Agonies in the Life of Oscar Wilde, pamphlet front cover (New York, 1882, illustrations by Chas. Kendrick)

And in Philadelphia, Wilde told the *Philadelphia Press*:

> Why, they might have great fields of callas growing there! Do you understand my line for lilies, and roses, and sunflowers? No? Oh, don't you know there is no flower so purely decorative as the sunflower. In the house it is perhaps too large and glaring. But how lovely a line of them are in a garden, against a wall, or massed in groups! Its form is perfect. . . . And you have such beautiful lilies in America. I've seen a new one that we do not have in England, that star-shaped lily. I always loved lilies. At Oxford I kept my room filled with them, and I had a garden of them, where I used to work very often.[3]

By the time Wilde reached San Francisco, there was a particularly heightened craze for sunflowers (FIG. 6). Local florists reported that they could not keep up with the demand for this newly favored flower. "In compliment to the Apostle of the Beautiful," Platte's Hall was filled with sunflowers for Wilde's appearance before a "select and fashionable audience," and a week after his departure, the Ivy Social Club "announced an Aesthetic Social—all males to wear knee breeches, ladies to carry sunflower fans which would also serve as programs."[4]

And all across the country he had captivated, sunflowers and lilies—the flowers Oscar Wilde had carried or worn in his lapel—bloomed on crazy quilts.

NOTES

1. *Ornamental Stitches for Embroidery* (Lynn, Mass.: T. E. Parker, 1885), unpaginated.
2. Mrs. Thomas Bailey Aldrich, *Crowding Memories* (London: Constable, 1921), p. 247.
3. Oscar Wilde, quoted in the *Philadelphia Press*, January 17, 1882, p. 2.
4. Lois Foster Rodecape, "Gilding the Sunflower: A Study of Oscar Wilde's Visit to San Francisco," *California Historical Society Quarterly* 19, no. 2 (June 1940): 97–112ff.

JOHN TAM'S CRAZY QUILTS

Stockton, California, late nineteenth century
Silk, satin, velvet, and plush; pressed,
embroidered, and embellished
Sizes unknown
Present location unknown

THERE WAS SURELY NO MORE EXTRAORDINARY CALIFORNIA quiltmaker than John Thomas Tam (1860–1896), but we know of his work only through two photographs and an album of miscellaneous newspaper clippings.[1] One of those clippings notes that "Monsieur Ravella," seen posed in embroidered elegance with an unidentified assistant (FIG. 1),

> is a Native Son of the Golden West [his parents had come to the gold fields in 1849] and up Stockton way where he comes from, they call him Jack Tam. He is tall and slender and good-looking, and has expressive purple eyes. Incidentally he eats fire and chews redhot-iron, molten lead and all that sort of thing for a livelihood. He also does plain and fancy juggling on the side.

FIGURE 1, OPPOSITE
"Monsieur Ravella" (John Tam) with an unidentified assistant, undated photograph, Allen Photographic Studio, Stockton, California *Holt-Atherton Special Collections*

FIGURE 2, ABOVE
John Tam's letterhead *Holt-Atherton Special Collections*

Tam's Stockton boyhood had been spent in the center of a town distinguished by myriad amusements: "literary readings, human exhibitions, dog and monkey shows, tableaus, dioramas, panoramas, acrobatics, conjurers, stereopticians, harpists, vocalists, recitations, Swiss bell ringers, operas, concerts, balls, ballet, pantomimes, statuary exhibitions, polytechnic entertainment, prestidigitators, illusionists, impersonations and scientific exhibits . . . phrenology and mesmerism."[2] By September 25, 1880, "Professor Tam" was juggling at Weber Hall (FIG. 2).

Continuing a varied career as an itinerant entertainer, Tam eventually joined the Pawnee Indian Medicine Company, and it was during this period that he found his creative moment:

> I did it to prevent myself dying of ennui. You see I was once in the dime museum business, and there, you know a fellow has to do his turn as often as a dozen, and

even fifteen times a day. There is not time to go home between acts, and it gets awfully monotonous in the dressing room. One day about a dozen years ago I had a bit of mending to do on some props. There was no girl to do it for me so I tackled the job myself. I found the time passed quickly while I was plying the needle, so for the fun of the thing I began to go in for fancy bits of patchwork for stage suits and things. Gradually the diversion became a passion.

There are hundreds of thousands of different pieces in the combination, every one of them silk or satin, and not a dozen over three inches square . . . with both sides matching and in perfect harmony. . . . Besides the time taken up it has cost me a trifle over $2,000 for materials. You see there are over sixty pounds of spangles in it, and spangles cost about $2 a pound. It takes three stitches to each spangle, and there are about 4,200 spangles to the pound. That would make about three-quarters of a million stitches for spangles alone, and the spangles are mere little extras.

Newspaper reporters were eager to add their own descriptive embellishment:

every seam is embroidered in fancy silk stitching, or with gold cord, and many of the larger pieces of work are either painted or embroidered in floral designs by the man himself. . . . It is composed of silk, plush and velvet . . . which with the gorgeous colors, gives the appearance of a magic cave. It is in patch work and of all kinds of designs, stars, hearts, squares, roses, diamonds, shells, fawns and numerous other designs all sowed by Mr. Ravella's hands....Monsieur Ravella bit off another length of silk and again commenced plying his needle. No woman could have been defter, no slave of the sweating system more industrious. He was working like an antebellum black, but as he only worked for the fun of the thing he was above all pity.

Together, John Tam and his obviously admiring journalistic observer set down a thorough description of the crazy quilt: the exquisite style, the demanding technique, the glorious materials, the marvelous minutia—the wonder of it all! Tam's passion was duplicated with variable competence and creativity across the United States:

> If one half of the old women in the United States who make crazy quilts for the fun of the thing and then grumble over the pastime, were to go in for the work with the same assiduity as does Monsieur Ravella there would be no room for anything besides crazy quilts in America. The place would gleam with them and glisten like a kaleidoscope even in the night time. ...Half creation would go mad were the sober monotony of an every day landscape transformed into the appalling diversity of Monsieur Ravella's crazy work.

John Tam's passion, and his pleasure, could not be restrained, and at some point he turned to the creation of what was surely his masterwork:

> When he goes on the stage his scenery—wings, drop scenes, tormentors and everything is composed of handsome crazy-quilt and embroidery work entirely of his own manufacture. His "props" and wardrobe are likewise the work of his own hands....He is now working on a stage outfit, including a drop scene, wings, and everything else necessary which when completed will entirely equip an ordinary thirty-five foot stage [FIG. 3].

The magnificence of his work combined with the magnitude of this incredible undertaking are even more remarkable when one considers that this was not the work of a long and otherwise idle lifetime: John Tam was only thirty-five when he died. He was remembered in his obituary as "a clever juggler."[3]

NOTES

1. John Tam's personal and professional lives have been meticulously chronicled by Janene Ford, Library/Archives Assistant at the Holt-Atherton Department of Special Collections at the University of the Pacific Library, in "Remnants of John Tam's Life and Career: Popular Entertainment and Medicine Shows, 1860–1896," *The Far-Westerner: The Quarterly Bulletin of the Stockton Corral of Westerners* 37, no. 3–4 (Fall/Winter 1996). All factual matters pertaining to John Tam that are cited in this entry are attributable to Ms. Ford's extensive research, and I am grateful for her academic generosity. All the quotations used here are quoted in Ms. Ford's article from the V. Covert Martin Papers, MSS 9, Holt-Atherton Department, University of the Pacific Libraries; Mr. Martin was John Tam's nephew.

2. Ford, "Remnants," pp. 8–9.

3. The costumes, the quilts, and especially the trappings for a thirty-five-foot stage—how could this all have vanished? A newspaper clipping, post 1893, tells of Tam's plans for a South American tour; if that was realized, could the work have been lost or sold there? Was it cut and reconfigured after his death? Did it all simply mold and rot for decades in unmarked boxes? Perhaps there is some small bit of his life tucked away, unidentified:

> Special notice was given the ladies after each performance ...to visit the hall during the day and they would see Mons. Ravella busy at his patch work....Many embraced the opportunity as many of our ladies here quilt and his work is in a different scale. All who visited him expressed themselves as delighted with his handywork. Several bought pin-cushions (as souvenirs which will serve to remember him when he is perhaps thousands of miles from here).

THE STORYBOOK QUILT

Possibly Utica, New York, ca. 1895
Made by Eudotia Sturgis Wilcox
Primarily silk and velvet; pressed, appliquéd, embroidered, and
embellished; glove leather, paint, watercolors, and ink
78 ¼ x 68 in. (198.8 x 172.7 cm)
Natural History Museum of Los Angeles County

THE INTELLECTUAL LIFE OF CALIFORNIA was formulated in its earliest years through the establishment of its public libraries; the first, a subscription library, was established in Monterey in 1849. It was a prominent location, both socially and politically; the seat of the Spanish government, Monterey next became the capital of Alta California under the Mexican Republic, and, finally, served as the seat of the first government when California passed into the hands of the United States. The community considered a library additionally important as a gathering place for young men. The Monterey Library Association's constitution determined that

> The design of this Association is through a Library and Reading Room, to afford amusement, entertainment and profit to a large class who, without its aid, would waste their time in the frivolities and questionable pastimes so prevalent in our State.[1]

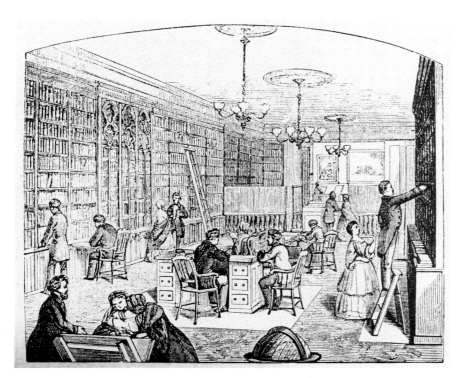

FIGURE I
"The Library and Reading Room of the Mercantile Library," *Hutching's Magazine* 4, no. 11 (May 1860)

Californians were increasingly about the business of duplicating the cultural institutions that had been a part of their eastern lives, and the early settlers were eventually joined in that undertaking by the miners who had read in their crude camps, many through loosely formed associations. The number of public libraries in the state grew rapidly between 1851 and 1855. By 1861, the Mercantile Library in San Francisco (FIG. 1) boasted an extensive and current collection; in addition to the classics, its 11,591 volumes included the first edition of Walt Whitman's *Leaves of Grass* and works by Hawthorne, Melville, and Harriet Beecher Stowe.[2]

Mrs. Stowe's *Uncle Tom's Cabin* (1852) also came to California on the detailed, storybook surface of the crazy quilt Eudotia Sturgis Wilcox had constructed for her grandchildren in New York. The tender scene Mrs. Wilcox chose to illustrate, Tom with Little Eva (FIG. 2), is the book's most popular, and it was used with variation by almost every illustrator in each of the book's numerous editions. It was also the image

The Storybook Quilt

FIGURE 2
The Storybook Quilt (detail)

NOTES

1. Hugh S. Baker, "Rational Amusements in Our Midst: Public Libraries in California, 1849–1859," *California Historical Society Quarterly* 38 (1959): 296.

2. Ibid., p. 301.

3. Illustrated in *Sotheby's Catalogue*, October 13, 2000, no. 19.

4. See Chapter Seven, "Literary Influences," in Sandi Fox, *Small Endearments: Nineteenth-Century Quilts for Children and Dolls* (Nashville, Tenn.: Rutledge Hill Press, 1994).

Mrs. Stowe chose when she commissioned a painting as a gift for her London publisher.[3]

Literary references and images appear on children's quilts throughout the nineteenth century,[4] but never with such illustrative invention. The patterns in all probability were taken from the books themselves, and they were translated into textiles with remarkable detail. The costumes on Heidi and her grandfather (FIG. 3), for example, are particularly fine. Heidi's skirt is made dimensional by careful folding and layering, and Grandfather's costume is perfect to the smallest detail: a tiny tassel on his cap; the delineation of the soles on his comfortable slippers; five white buttons formed by French knots on each side of his knee breeches; a bit of cuff showing beneath the sleeve of his brown velvet jacket; the bit of metallic thread forming his watch chain; a small piece of green ribbon constituting a tie above his white vest. Throughout the quilt, the faces of the figures are constructed from soft glove leather on which features have been painted. The hands are of glove leather as well, allowing for the realistic contouring of the hand in which Grandfather holds his clay pipe.

Uncle Remus is readily recognizable, as is a scene from *Little Women*, but a westering scene (FIG. 4) remains an unidentified illustration from one of the extensive number of books written celebrating America's greatest adventure.

FIGURE 3
The Storybook Quilt (detail)

FIGURE 4
The Storybook Quilt (detail)

THE CITRUS QUILT

Riverside, California, 1893
Made by Eliza S. (Mrs. E. M.) Sheldon
Silk, satin and velvet; pieced, embroidered, and embellished
74 x 74 in. (188.1 x 188.1 cm)
Riverside Municipal Museum

IN 1868, THE CALIFORNIA SILK CENTER ASSOCIATION purchased about 8,600 acres in Southern California. The land was intended for the establishment of a colony based on the silkworm culture and the development of a silk industry that would take advantage of the currently state-sanctioned silk craze. Before the boom collapsed, California was paying bounties of $250 for the planting of 5,000 mulberry trees and $300 for every hundred million cocoons produced.[1] But it was another colony that would settle the area, and orange trees rather than mulberry that would eventually thrive there.

In Knoxville, Tennessee, in March 1870, J. W. North announced his intention to organize a colony for settlement in Southern California. In a leaflet sent to potential participants he wrote:

FIGURE 1
The Citrus Quilt (detail)

Appreciating the advantages of associated settlement, we aim to secure at least 100 good families, who can invest $1000 each, in the purchase of land; while at the same time we earnestly invite all good, industrious people to join us, who can, by investing a smaller amount, contribute in any degree to the general prosperity.... We wish to form a colony of intelligent, industrious, and enterprising people, so that each one's industry will help to promote his neighbor's interests, as well as his own.[2]

Among the "intelligent, industrious, and enterprising people" who settled Riverside in 1870 were optimists from Belle Plain, Iowa, and from Upper New York State. Eliza S. Sheldon (1825–1896), her husband, and their sons Fred, Ezra, and Otis, also shared the vision. More than two decades later it was Eliza, then a woman of sixty-eight, who embroidered the symbol of the community's, and the state's, eventual prosperity—the orange—in the center of her masterwork (FIG. 1).

Shortly after settling, the pioneers were joined by "a coterie of spiritualists and free thinkers, rather clannish in their ways."[3] Spiritualists eventually became a substantial minority in the community and it was a member of that group, another Eliza (Mrs. Luther Tibbets), who

The Citrus Quilt

introduced the navel orange to Riverside, probably in 1875. The finest table
orange, the Washington navel was distinctively flavored and seedless—and it
was a horticultural triumph.

By the 1880s the orange, like North's leaflet, had become a promotional
factor in the efforts to encourage settlement in California. The Ontario
Observer reported:

> In the cultivation of fruit (the most charming, healthful and lucrative of occupa-
> tions, and decidedly the most fascinating) are to be found men from every walk of
> life. They have come from every State in the Union and from every Province of
> Canada, and not a few from the Old World. These men left the judge's bench and
> the banker's office, the editorial chair, the merchant's counter and the accoun-
> tant's desk, and the use of the lancet, the farm and the factory, the mechanic's
> tools and the professor's toga, for a more congenial occupation and a congenial
> clime. They found both—and more.[4]

And they came (FIG. 2).

The orange crate labels that appeared in the 1880s and 1890s served to
spread a romanticized version of California and were probably the inspiration
for the central image on Eliza Sheldon's magnificent quilt. Eliza's orange is
bounded by California poppies and by sprays of the area's pepper tree (see
FIG. 1); identifiable botanical images are planted across the entire quilt. She did
not yield to the wild abandon of a crazed, asymmetrical background; Eliza's
embroidered tour de force is worked over the simple, classic, pieced patterns

FIGURE 3
The Citrus Quilt (detail)

FIGURE 4
The Citrus Quilt (detail)

FIGURE 5
The Citrus Quilt (detail)

that she probably stitched, as a young woman, in cotton dress goods. Stars (FIGS. 3 and 4) were particular favorites; simple squares and diamonds and hexagons proved popular foils for floral motifs, and she executed a particularly elegant basket (FIG. 5). The visual impact is staggering, but it is at heart a very orderly presentation, neatly bordered and sashed, and finished with a crocheted edging (FIG. 6).

Riverside's famed Washington navel received gold medals at horticultural exhibitions in such events as the New Orleans World Fair in 1884. But Eliza modestly contented herself with the ribbons awarded to her *Citrus Quilt* at early local fairs.

NOTES

1. Tom Patterson, *A Colony for California* (Riverside, Calif.: The Museum Press, 1996), p. 35.
2. J. W. North, "A Colony for California," leaflet, Knoxville, Tenn., March 17, 1870. North's associate, Dr. James P. Greves, coordinated his own efforts from Marshall, Michigan.
3. Elmer Wallace Holmes, *History of Riverside County, California* (Los Angeles: History Record Company, 1912), p. 38.
4. Quoted in Claire Perry, *Pacifica Arcadia: Images of California 1600–1915* (New York and Oxford: The Oxford University Press, 1999), p. 91.

FIGURE 6
The Citrus Quilt (detail)

THE MORE FAMILY QUILT

Oakland, California, marked 1893
Made by the More family children
Velvet and satin; embroidered
76 x 74 in. (193 x 188 cm)
Collection of the Oakland Museum of California

IN 1893, THE FIVE CHILDREN IN THE MORE FAMILY (four boys and one girl) embroidered this splendid bedcover as a Christmas present for their grandmother. In wool and cotton floss, on sixteen alternating black and wine-colored velvet squares, the children, working under the supervision of their mother, rendered images from the Oakland farm on which they lived.

A young boy strides among what must have been intended to represent the farm's bountiful orchards (FIG. 1). The horticultural possibilities in that area were extolled in romantic detail in a book on Alameda County, published in 1883:

> Here a slope, basking in the full sunshine, fit to distill the sugar-essence of grapes; there a low, moist, cool valley, the home of the apple and plum; or a rich, mellow, alluvial soil, sheltered, cozy and warm, where the peach blushes as a rose ...[1]

Flowers were planted across the surface—in simple outline stitches worked from commercial stamped patterns, in giant sprays with colorful buds on the tips of long splayed and thorny stems, and as small single blossoms tucked away in little corners. Birds fly among the flowers; seven perch stiffly around the outer edge of a huge clock that announces it is one o'clock. Several other clocks and pocket watches appear (set for differing times), as do a number of horseshoes—typical of the spot motifs found on crazy quilts of the period. The vignette of tea being poured is identical to a design found on grannies' kitchen towels throughout the country (FIG. 2).

Farm animals appear in scattered profusion: cows and horses, sheep, and the very fattest of pigs. Cats and small dogs wander at will, but among them all, three large working dogs (prominently identified as Bruno, Uno [FIG. 3], and Count) seem to stand guard over the barnyard. But giants among them all are the cocks of the walk, their fierce profiles stitched on the most colorful and elaborately worked block of this utterly charming undertaking (FIG. 4).

FIGURE 1
The More Family Quilt (detail)

The More Family Quilt

FIGURE 2
The More Family Quilt (detail)

FIGURE 3
The More Family Quilt (detail)

NOTE

1. The horticultural description continued, noting that, "The choicest varieties of grapes grow to perfection," and assuring the reader that should he choose to come to prosper in Alameda County, "... from five to twenty acres on each farm, planted with fruit suitable for drying, raisins or wine, will make a gradual transit from the old ways of farming, without jeopardizing present sources of income ..." and that he would be "certain of pecuniary profit"; see *History of Alameda County, California* (Oakland, Calif.: M. W. Wood, 1883), p. 37. Similar books were published for most California counties during this same period. Almost uniformly they covered geology, topography, soil, and productions; early history and settlement; names of the early pioneers and incidents of pioneer life; political history; and separate histories of the townships, sketches of early and prominent citizens, listings of churches, schools, secret societies, etc. Expressions of county and community pride, these publications also were intended to encourage settlement and promote development.

FIGURE 4
The More Family Quilt (detail)

THE CIGAR RIBBONS QUILT

Durham, Butte County, California, ca. 1900
Attributed to a member of the Goss family
Silk and cotton; applied and embroidered
70½ x 70⅛ in. (179.1 x 178.1 cm)
Collection of the California State Parks,
Bidwell Mansion State Park

CAMPED TEN MILES PAST A "PRETTY OAK GROVE," Ruth Shackleford recorded in her 1868 diary that "The men have made up a big fire and are all standing around it nearly crazy because they are out of tobacco. Some of them have chewed sticks till their teeth are sore."[1] In describing the stores and provisions necessary for an overland expedition, *The Prairie Traveler* had anticipated such a situation:

> at a time when men are performing the severest labor that the human system is capable of enduring, [the absence of tobacco] was a great privation. In this destitute condition we found a substitute for tobacco in the bark of the red willow. . . . The outer bark is first removed with a knife, after which the inner bark is scraped up into ridges around the sticks and held in the fire until it is thoroughly roasted, when it is taken off the stick, pulverized in the hand, and is ready for smoking. It has the narcotic properties of the tobacco, and is quite agreeable to the taste and smell.[2]

The cigar smoker was an established presence in the West. Soldiers returned to the East from the 1846–47 war in Mexico with a great appreciation for the superior quality of the Mexican-Spanish cigar. Californios were heavy smokers (FIG. 1), a habit not lost on the increasing numbers coming west with the annexation of California in 1848 and the discovery of gold.[3]

Prior to 1870, a manufactured cigar would have been a purchase of some extravagance, but by the 1880s, in parlor and saloon, the cigar was the country's most popular tobacco product, reaching the peak of consumption in 1907. By the turn of the century, more than 350,000 brands were in production[4]; the silk ribbons (approximately .2 cm wide) with which they were tied into bundles identified the manufacturer. Those bright bits of silk, both practical and promotional, proved absolutely irresistible to American needleworkers; they began to catalogue cigar ribbons into parlor throws and a variety of smaller objects such as pillows and tablecovers.

Late-nineteenth-century quiltmakers of this period were caught up in the asymmetrical aspects of crazy quilts, but the use of cigar ribbons required that originality be expressed only in endless geometric variation (FIG. 2), with the embellishment of the seams almost always restricted to simple feather or herringbone stitches. Some needleworkers would have nothing to do with what they considered this lesser challenge. In an 1884 short story in *Godey's Lady's Book*, young Heloise Herbert and her friend Marie determined they each would begin a crazy quilt. In a letter discussing her search for bits of silk and brocade, Heloise writes of her delight with one recent contribution—"Tom Lee has

The Cigar Ribbons Quilt

FIGURE 2
Maker unidentified, *Cigar Ribbons Bedcover*, provenance unknown,
ca. 1900, applied and embroidered silk,
76 x 56½ in. (193 x 143.5 cm)
Collection of the Los Angeles County Museum of Art, gift of Clarence Fleming

FIGURE 3
The Cigar Ribbons Quilt (detail)

given me a lovely silk handkerchief he has only carried a few times. Wasn't it sweet of him?"—and her displeasure with another—"Ned is such an absurd brother! This morning he came in with a lot of those nasty little yellow cigar ribbons, all in a tangle, and offered them to me for my crazy quilt."[5]

The collection of cigar ribbons in numbers sufficient to complete a substantial project usually required that the effort be expanded beyond one's own household. Fortunately for Mrs. Elizabeth Poyser, her son and son-in-law operated cigar stores in Ellensburg and Seattle, Washington[6]; Sadie Coe's husband

FIGURE 4
The Cigar Ribbons Quilt (detail)

traveled throughout the Pacific Northwest and persuaded the cigar stores and hotels he frequented to save their cigar ribbons for his wife.[7]

The remarkable variety of the ribbons in this fragile and faded artifact (FIG. 3) suggests that its maker must surely have gone beyond the personal preferences of the smokers in her own household. Londres and Blackstone were brands seen in large numbers on cigar ribbon pieces across the country; the brands here are drawn from an abundance of seldom-seen ribbons. In addition to the requisite ladies' names such as Molly Stark and Mollie Darling, Eva Tanguay (a great vaudeville star of the period), Thelma, Dorothy, Elaine, and Clara, these bear wonderfully jolly and inventive phrases:

American Belle	Love Watches
Blue Head	Mark of Honor
Bull Dog	My Sweet Heart
Dancing Hussars	Paid in Full
Dandies	Red Car
Evening Dreams	Silver Eagle
High Life	Under Southern Skies
Lonesome Town	

Because the piece was worked in, and descended through, an early Durham, California, pioneer family, there is a particular pleasure in reading brand names with a decidedly western flavor: Sharpshooters and Sheriff Bell, Cabaleros and the Old Homestead, Pacific, Golden Gate, and California (FIG. 4)!

When the quiltmaker's collection of cigar ribbons was exhausted (and perhaps herself as well!), she bound off her bedcover with a soft, corded braid punctuated with festive floral tassels at each corner (FIG. 5).

NOTES

1. Quoted in Kenneth L. Holmes, ed., *Covered Wagon Women: Diaries & Letters from the Western Trails, 1840–1900*, vol. 9 (Glendale, Calif. and Spokane, Wash.: The Arthur H. Clark Company, 1990), p. 198.

2. Captain Randolph B. Marcy, *The Prairie Traveler: A Hand-book for Overland Expeditions* (Washington, D.C.: War Department, 1859), pp. 34–35. Crude construction had, in fact, characterized the homemade products of the early tobacco trade. Almost every farmhouse had a tobacco patch, large or small—and almost everyone in that farm family chewed or smoked. From their own leaves, farmers rolled their own cigars and production that exceeded personal use became a staple on the Yankee peddler's wagon; see Robert K. Heimann, *Tobacco and Americans* (New York: McGraw-Hill, 1960), p. 87.

3. Heimann, *Tobacco and Americans*, p. 89.

4. *Better Choose Me*, exhibition brochure (North Newton, Kans.: Kaufman Museum, 1999).

5. Dulcie Weir, "The Career of a Crazy Quilt," *Godey's Lady's Book* 109 (July 1884): 78.

6. Mrs. Poyser's cigar ribbon throw (82 ½ x 73 ½ in.) is illustrated in Diana McLachlan, *A Common Thread: Quilts in the Yakima Valley* (Yakima, Wash.: Yakima Valley Museum & Historical Association, 1985), p. 50.

7. Mrs. Coe's cigar ribbon throw (77 x 55 in.) is illustrated in Joyce Gross, *A Patch in Time*, (Mill Valley, Calif.: Mill Valley Quilt Authority, 1973), p. 26.

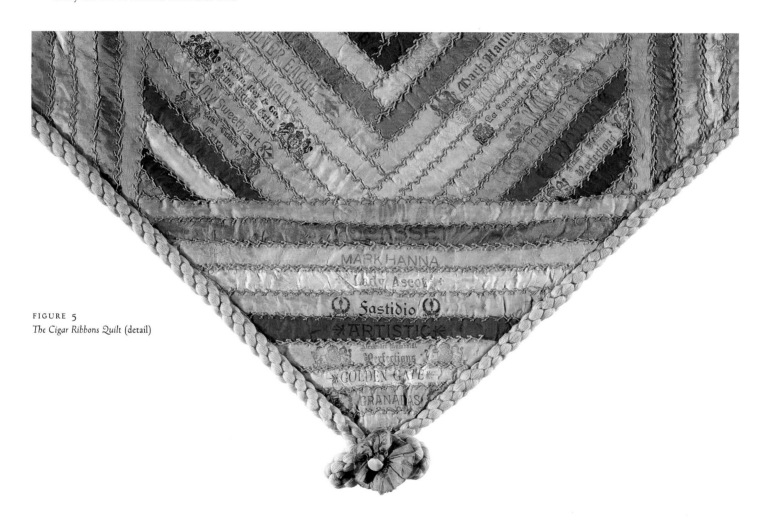

FIGURE 5
The Cigar Ribbons Quilt (detail)

PART 6

"I See by Your Outfit That You Are a Cowboy"

*E*VEN BEFORE THE REVOLUTIONARY WAR, adventurous Americans had begun to detach themselves from the eastern seaboard; it was a modest movement in the beginning, along little more than pathways, with the great river systems determining the routes of internal migration. By 1800, settlers were moving deep into the Mississippi Valley. These were formidable frontiers; as late as 1838, an English traveler stood on the edge of the forest at the Mississippi River and later wrote:

> A few miles farther on, we went ashore at the wooding-place, and I had my first walk in the trodden forest. The height of the trees seemed incredible, as we stood at their foot, and looked up. It made us feel suddenly dwarfed. We stood in a crowd of locust and cotton-wood trees, elm, maple and live oak: and they were all bound together by an inextricable tangle of creepers, which seemed to forbid our penetrating many paces into the forest beyond where the wood cutters had intruded.[1]

Then, in 1845, the editor of the New York *Morning News*, John L. O'Sullivan, added a significant phrase to the American vocabulary by advising his reading public that it was "our manifest destiny to overspread and to possess the whole of the continent . . . for the great experiment of liberty"; it was the vision Thomas Jefferson had held. Western expansion became a patriotic preoccupation, and Manifest Destiny was realized with extraordinary speed with the rapid acquisition of large areas of new land: Texas in 1845, Oregon in 1846, California in 1848 (by secession from Mexico), and additional segments of the Southwest in 1853 (through the Gadsden Purchase). The migration that began so slowly on foot ended in a fevered rush to the Pacific Ocean.

In his 1893 address to a meeting of the American Historical Society, "The Significance of the American Frontier in American History," historian Frederick Jackson Turner (1861–1932) defined the westward movement and the receding frontier as significant in the formation of the American character. Now, just as the eagle and Lady Liberty had identified us as a nation, the log cabin and the American cowboy came to define the American West—and the American quiltmaker had new subjects for inspiration and illustration.

NOTE

1. Harriet Martineau, *Retrospect of Western Travel*, 1838, quoted in Ralph K. Andrist, ed., *The American Heritage History of the Making of a Nation* (New York: American Heritage Publishing Co., Inc., 1968), p. 163.

THE "LOG CABIN" QUILT

Provenance unknown, late nineteenth century
Quiltmaker unknown
Cotton; pieced and quilted
74 x 73 in. (188 x 185.4 cm)
Collection of Herb Wallerstein

THE LOG CABIN WAS A UNIQUE ARCHITECTURAL ADAPTATION of the traditional dwelling brought to the Delaware Valley by Swedish settlers in the middle of the seventeenth century; it was this primitive structure that facilitated America's rapid expansion across the continent. Faced with providing shelter for his family in hostile, wooded surroundings, one man with a single-bitted axe could clear the site he had selected; bark, shape, and notch the logs; make skids to position the logs into place; cut shakes for the roof; and—without nails, which were too heavy and expensive to carry with him—erect, in short order, a cabin sufficient for his immediate needs. The log cabin understandably came to be synonymous with self-sufficiency, a quality highly prized by the American moving west.[1]

During the height of westward expansion, even if she herself were not a physical participant in that grand adventure, letters and reports from the trail and popular literature of the period assured that the quiltmaker was kept abreast of the activities and the images of the frontier. She eventually constructed her own "log cabin," seen by many as the quintessential American quilt. The classic geometric variations of the "log cabin" quilt are abstractions carrying appropriate pattern names such as "Straight Furrow" and "Barn-Raising," but this sweet variation is a somewhat more literal design; it

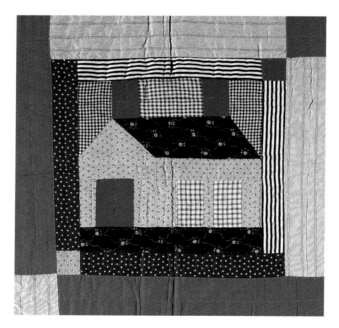

FIGURE 1
The "Log Cabin" Quilt (detail)

combines a classic pieced-house pattern (FIG. 1) with elements of a log cabin pattern variation (FIG. 2). It is reminiscent of a delightful illustration (FIG. 3) in the 1876 memoirs of a Michigan pioneer, William Nowlin, who remembered vividly the frontier of his childhood: "We were on the border of civilization."[2]

The quilt recalls, also, the image of a log cabin captured by the most significant of America's early foreign visitors, Alexis De Tocqueville (1831–32):

> The dwelling in which the emigrants live has no internal division and no store-house. The whole family comes to seek shelter of an evening in the single room which it contains. This dwelling forms as it were a little world of its own. It is an ark of civilization lost in the middle of an ocean of leaves, it is sort of an oasis in the desert. A hundred paces beyond it is the everlasting forest stretching its shade around it and solitude begins again.[3]

The "Log Cabin" Quilt

FIGURE 2
The "Log Cabin" Quilt (detail)

FIGURE 3
Artist unknown, untitled black-and-
white illustration, in *The Bark Covered
House; or, Back in the Woods Again*

The California trail would be truly opened only when emigrants had suc-
cessfully taken wagons across the Sierra Nevadas. After unsuccessful attempts
by the Bartleson Party in 1841 and the Chiles-Walker Party in 1843 (all their
wagons had to be abandoned and they crossed into California on horseback
and on foot), the crossing with wagons was finally accomplished by several
members of the Stevens Party, probably on November 25, 1844. Six of the
eleven wagons that had survived the overland journey had been abandoned earlier, with their contents, in the snow at a lake in the mountains; three young
men were left to guard them. At the lower end of the lake, they set about at
once to build a log cabin. In two days they had erected a 12 x 14-foot cabin,
which they roofed with pine boughs. A large log chimney, built at one end of
the cabin, was faced on the inside, with stones. There were no windows and an
opening served as a door, and they kept themselves warm with bedding gathered from the wagons they were guarding.[4] This log cabin would stand to
house other emigrants; the Breen family in 1846, as part of the Donner Party,
took refuge there during that dreadful winter. It was the type of small, sturdy
structure that dotted the landscape all the way to California.

NOTES

1. The log cabin suggested qualities of charac-
    ter that were used to great political advan-
    tage, particularly in the presidential
    campaign of 1840. The successful Whig
    candidate, William Henry Harrison, pre-
    sented himself as one of the "common
    people," having humble beginnings in a log
    cabin, which, with a jug of cider, became
    the symbol for his campaign; he had, in
    fact, been born in a mansion in tidewater
    Virginia.
2. William Nowlin, *The Bark Covered House;
    or, Back in the Woods Again* (Chicago: The
    Lakeside Press, 1937). p. 341. Originally
    printed for the author in Detroit, 1876.
3. Alexis De Tocqueville, *Journey to America*
    (New Haven: Yale University Press, 1960),
    p. 341.
4. George R. Stewart, *The California Trail*
    (New York: McGraw-Hill, 1962), p. 75.

THE COWBOYS QUILT

California; blocks completed in 1933, quilted in 1953
Made by Thelma Norman Ryan
Silk, sateen, cotton, and wool; appliquéd, embroidered,
painted, and quilted
88 x 71 in (223.5 x 180.3 cm)
Autry Museum of Western Heritage

FIGURE 1
The Cowboys Quilt (detail)

THELMA RYAN (1908–1987) TRACED HER IMAGES of the American cowboy (FIG. 1) from the covers of western pulp magazines; they had been drawn by a group of prolific illustrators with clear aesthetic directives:

> They had to have action, color, six-shooter spitting fire, hero in trouble, but not defeated, and no girl kissing![1]

The quiltmaker adapted nineteen magazine covers (three are repeated or reversed) into cotton and wool, silk and sateen, and in exquisite detail she illustrated all the major elements of a cowboy's outfit. Could she have known of the origins of those familiar costumes?

From the beginning, much of the cowboy's dress was taken from that of the Mexican *vaquero*. In the early 1840s, John Bidwell, newly arrived in California,

> saw through the door a man whom, from his light hair, I took to be an American, although he was clad in the wild picturesque garb of a native Californian, including serape and the huge spurs used by the vaquero.[2]

The *vaquero* had worn leather leggings to protect himself from the cactus and the chaparral of the Southwest; the Anglo-American cowboy climbed into the earliest of those seatless coverings, shotgun *chaperajos*. Many riders came to prefer "batwing" chaps, those leggings that wrapped around and fastened in the back and could be put on without taking off boots and spurs. Batwing chaps are

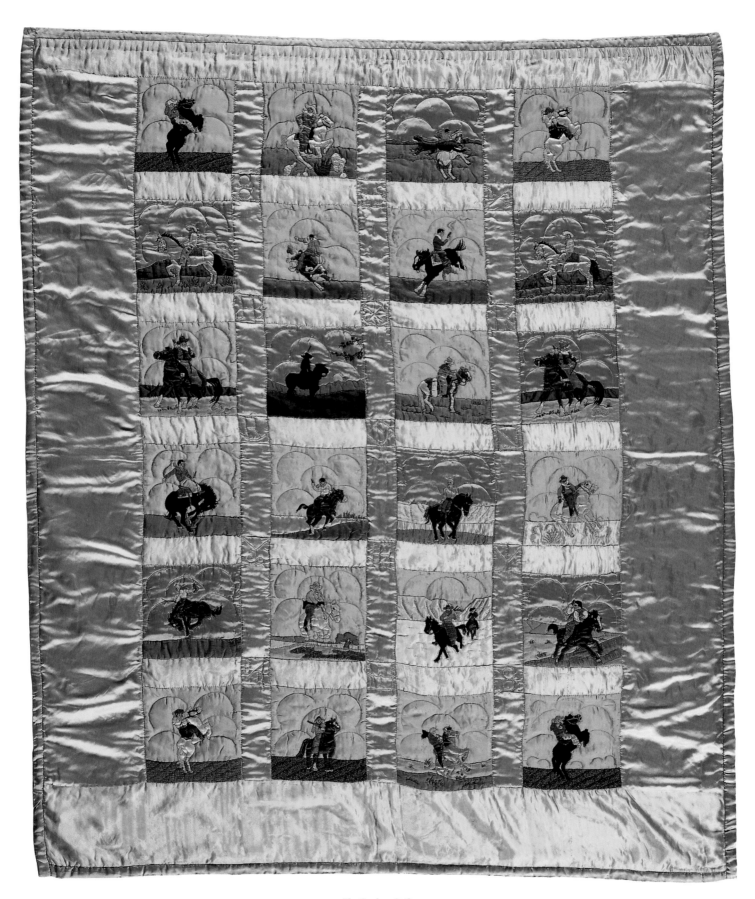

The Cowboys Quilt

FIGURE 2
The Cowboys Quilt (detail)

illustrated on blocks throughout the quilt, and many are clearly decorated with *conchos*, small, semi-flat circular disks usually made of silver (see FIG. 1).

The wide-brimmed hat (FIG. 2, top) was another significant *vaquero* contribution to cowboy dress, although the brim eventually narrowed somewhat. Several of the most popular styles appear on the quilt, including the Montana peak's four-sided crown, the classic Carlsbad crease, and the famous Stetson "Boss of the Plains." In Texas, in the 1860s, the cowboy who drove the half-wild longhorns was probably dressed in the "dilapidated remnants of a Confederate uniform, army-issue marching boots and a floppy woolen hat whose brim was pinned up by thorns."[3]

The twenty or thirty years that followed the Civil War were the cowboys' heydays, and by the time of the great 1886 Montana roundup the standard garb for American cowboys had been set. Through popular literature, the drawings of Frederic Remington (1861–1909), Wild West shows, and cowboy ballads ("I see by your outfit that you are a cowboy"), it was soon identifiable the whole world over. The cowboy eventually would replace the frontiersman as the primary—and idealized—image of the American West.

Turn-of-the-century ads proclaimed that "All over the West they wear Levi Strauss & Co.'s copper riveted overalls," but Levi's were not found regularly on the range until the 1920s. The cowboy's choice in the 1880s was woolen California pants, often striped or checked, although Teddy Blue Abbott preferred light gray, declaring them to be "the best pants ever made to ride in."[4]

The cowboy's shirt was long-sleeved, usually made with a three-to-five-button placket; in the nineteenth century, shirts were collarless and easily accommodated the bandanna, "the cowboy's best friend." The bandanna (FIG. 3) was used by the cowboy to ward off the dust of the trail, wash his face in cool water, tie up his broken bones and act as a tourniquet in case of snake bite, and hide his identity if he took to robbing trains or banks. He liked to wear a vest (its pockets proved handy places in which to carry a pouch of Bull Durham and his tally book and pencil) and often pulled on a pair of buckskin gauntlets (modeled on the gloves worn by the U.S. Cavalry) (FIG. 2, bottom).

Particular attention was paid to the cowboy's boots. The earliest were those brought home from the Civil War, flat heeled and round toed. It was soon discovered that a pointed toe would more easily slip into the stirrups, and a high heel prevented the foot from going too far forward. That high heel was

> a mark of distinction, the sign that the one wearing it is a riding man, and a riding man has always held himself above the man on foot. . . . When a man is seen wearing old boots so frazzled he can't strike a match on 'em without burnin' his feet, he is considered worthless and without pride.[5]

FIGURE 3
The Cowboys Quilt (detail)

FIGURE 4
The Cowboys Quilt (detail)

FIGURE 5
The Cowboys Quilt (detail)

FIGURE 6
George F. Gardner in woolie chaps,
undated sepia tone photograph,
photographer unidentified *Courtesy of the
Autry Museum of Western Heritage*

FIGURE 7
The Cowboys Quilt (detail)

Practical for his work, essential to his image, and rarely taken off, the spur fit over the back of the boot. Fancy dress spurs were highly admired, with jinglebobs—attached to a round revolving disk at the end of the spur (a rowel)—making noise as he ambled along. But the plainest spur, with a simple, star-shaped rowel, was the style most often worn; it is the style seen throughout the quilt (FIG. 4).

One block in particular (FIG. 5) demonstrates the completeness of each illustrated costume. Two cowboys are riding across a snowy northern range. The lead rider is, of course, wearing his Stetson. His shirt is a classic bib- or shield-front style, and around his neck is the omnipresent bright red bandanna, or "wipe." Most distinctively, he is wearing a pair of woolie chaps (FIG. 6), a piece of wintertime gear (a wooly is a sheep; woolies are chaps with the Angora hair left on). Here they are wonderfully approximated with embroidered stitches.

The cowboy took immense pride in his appearance, and once he had donned his identifiable garb, this "prairie knight" cut a very fine figure indeed. The quiltmaker took great care in selecting illustrations that presented the cowboy—and his horse—to best advantage. She also showed his guns, both holstered and blazing, and in a beautifully silhouetted vignette (FIG. 7) his girl. But "no girl kissing!"

NOTES

1. Raphael DeSoto, quoted in John A. Dinan, *The Pulp Western: A Popular History of the Western Fiction Magazine in America* (San Bernardino, Calif.: Borgo Press, 1983), pp. 110–11. DeSoto produced cover art for pulps such as *Dime Western, Ace Western, Red Seal Western, Star Western,* and *Western Story.* Street & Smith's weekly *Western Story* set the standards for this category of fiction, and its September 29, 1934, issue, along with the pattern tracings for her quilt blocks, accompanied Thelma Ryan's quilt when it was acquired by the Autry Museum of Western Heritage.

2. John Bidwell, "Life in California before the Gold Discovery," *The Century Magazine* 61, no. 2 (December 1890): 165. The man he saw was indeed an American—Thomas Bowen—"a resident of the Pueble of San Jose."

3. William H. Forbis, *The Cowboys* (New York: Time-Life Books, 1973), p. 20.

4. Holly George-Warren and Michelle Freedman, *How the West Was Worn* (New York: Harry N. Abrams in association with the Autry Museum of Western Heritage, Los Angeles, 2001), p. 33. See also William Manns and Elizabeth Clair Flood, *Cowboys & The Trappings of the Old West* (Santa Fe, N. Mex.: Zon International Publishing Company, 1997).

5. Ramon Adams, quoted in Winfred Blevins, *Dictionary of the American West* (New York: Facts on File, 1993) p. 95.

THE SACRAMENTO VALLEY SUGAN

Sacramento Valley, California, late nineteenth century
Maker unidentified
Wool; appliquéd and quilted
77 x 66 in. (195.6 x 167.6 cm)
Collection of the California State Parks, Sutter's Fort

FIGURE I
The Sacramento Valley Sugan (back,
detail)

THE MOST ELEMENTAL QUILT can also be the most enigmatic; so it is with this well-worn artifact. The simple, requisite units of construction are present: top, batting, and back. Two widths of a coarse red wool were worn and mended before they were sewn together to form the surface of the quilt. That surface was then strangely embellished with three vertical rows of large, dark shapes; although these could possibly suggest an unidentified ethnicity, it seems more probable that they were a rough attempt to illustrate the design elements of local cattle brands. The thick wool batting confirms the quilt's utilitarian intention, and the presence and patterns of substantial wear and deterioration on the striped backing (FIG. I) support the suspicion that this Sacramento Valley textile was used as a working cowboy's sugan (bedquilt).[1]

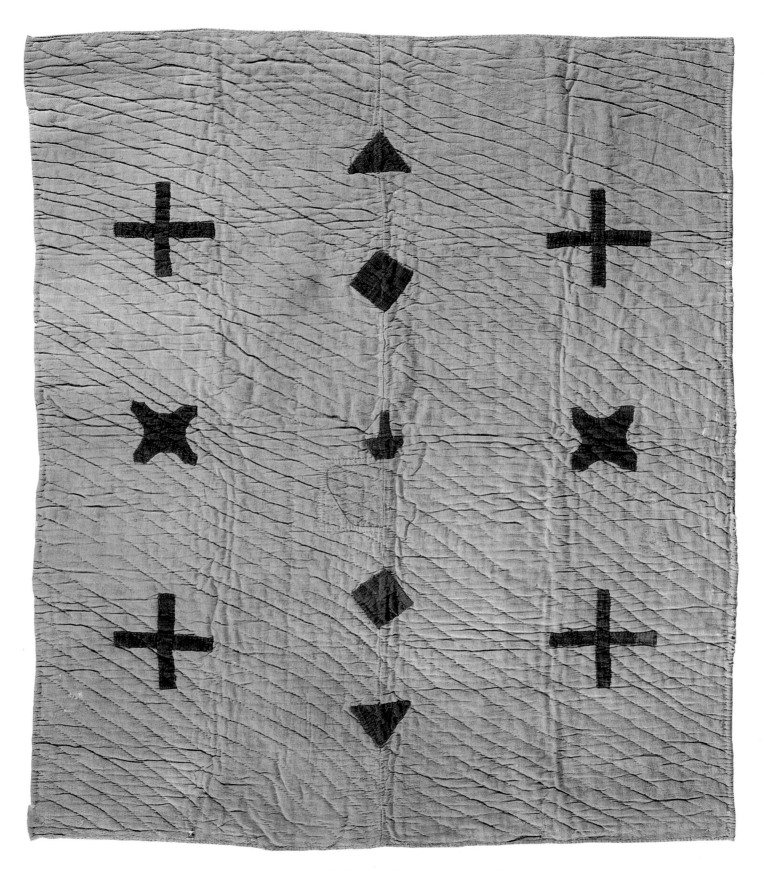

The Sacramento Valley Sugan

FIGURE 2
Ranch hands at the W. D. Boyce Cattle
Company in Kansas *Courtesy of the
Colorado Historical Society*

Because thickness was required for warmth, the cowboy's sugan was often a comforter (top, heavy batting, and back, tied together by knotted bits of yarn), such as the one covering a ranch hand bedding down for the night at the W. D. Boyce Cattle Company in Kansas (FIG. 2). This sugan was quilted, however, in slightly curving parallel lines set about 1½ inches apart; the thickness of the wool and the batting allowed only for large, crude quilting stitches, about three stitches per inch. Sugans usually were made of wool or denim, often from patches cut from discarded pants or coats; they were extremely heavy, usually weighing about four pounds—according to the cowboys, "a pound for each corner."[2] The quilt was often used as a mattress, inflicting substantial wear (as here) on the reverse.

Agnes Morley Cleaveland was born on a cattle ranch in New Mexico in 1874, and years later she set down vivid recollections of her life there and of the cowboys on that open range. The cowboy would arrive at the spring and fall roundups with his bulky and all-inclusive bedroll carried on his packhorse:

It probably inventoried a seven-by-sixteen-foot tarpaulin cover, a pair or two of store blankets, although in my day [she was writing in 1941] homemade comforters were in general use, a few "boughten soogins," things that "drove cowboys crazy" trying to decide which was length and which was breadth, as the saying went. I don't know how the word "soogin" came to mean bedquilt but I do know that the cheap ones were square and not quite adequate....Along with the soogins, the bedroll probably contained an extra pair of boots, socks, an extra shirt, smoking tobacco, and any other oddments making up the quota of personal belongings.[3]

The sugan was an essential part of the cowboy's bedroll, and the bedroll was an essential part of the cowboy's outfit. In addition to the sugan's weight and warmth, Agnes remembered:

It was a popular joke with us to tell some tenderfoot that we were very sorry, but we had to confess that all our beds had soogins in them, and then watch the look of apprehension settle in the visitor's eye.

One visitor put a certain cowboy properly in his place—an especially ignorant cowboy, I confess, but not too rare a specimen. The cowboy had laughed uproariously at the visitor's unconcealed distaste for sleeping in a bed infested with soogins.

"You should laugh," retorted the visitor. "I happen to know that you slumber in your bed."

The cowboy turned purple. "No man can say that about me and git off with it!" he roared.

Fortunately he had no gun. We rescued the visitor.[4]

Cowboying was usually a bachelor's business, and the sugan usually was made by female kin. Was this faded, worn bedquilt saved as a rough recollection of those independent days?

NOTES

1. Also spelled soogan, suggin, and sougan, the term—as with so many Western phrases—may well have come north from Texas, but was probably an Irish adaptation; see Winfred Blevins, *Dictionary of the American West* (New York: Facts on File, 1993) p. 351. "Cowboy" was, in fact, the word for the young boys who tended cattle in medieval Ireland.

2. Ramon F. Adams, *Western Words: A Dictionary of the American West* (Norman: University of Oklahoma Press, 1968), p. 311.

3. Agnes Morley Cleaveland, *No Life for a Lady* (Lincoln: University of Nebraska Press, 1977), pp. 165–66.

4. Ibid., p. 166.

THE BRANDS QUILT

Santa Maria Valley, California, ca. 1935
Made by Mrs. Burke
Cotton; pieced, embroidered, and quilted
83 x 68 in. (210.8 x 172.7 cm)
Private collection

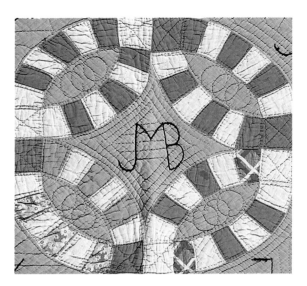

IN THE SIXTEENTH CENTURY, the Spanish conquistador Hernando Cortes took a small herd of cattle with him into Mexico; he had burned crosses into their hides, providing yet another custom for the *vaqueros* to eventually pass on to American cowboys. An intricate calligraphy was developed to brand the cows and calves, "the key to ownership in a business where ownership was everything."[1]

Brands were eventually compiled into commercially produced books, both regional and state, that provided valuable references as the number of ranges and ranches grew. An excellent example is *The Stock Manual*, which contains the "name, postoffice address, ranch location, marks and brands of all the principal stockmen of Western and North-western Texas, showing marks and brands on electrotype cuts as they appear on the animal."[2]

More modestly, cowboys on roundup often carried small notebooks listing the brands they might be encountering. In this tradition, in the open spaces formed by her pieced quilt pattern, an elusive Mrs. Burke (born 1885) recorded twenty-seven brands from the Santa Maria Valley in California (FIGS. 1 and 2); most prominent is that of the ERN (Ernest Righetti-Nunney) Ranch (FIG. 3).

Although many cowhands could neither read nor write, even the newest of them soon became adept at picking literally hundreds of brands out of a moving herd. The branding alphabet had three primary elements: letters, numbers, and variations, such as the Running W, the Rocking 7 (and the Swinging 7, Flying 7, Walking 7, and the Dragging 7), the Barbed Y, and the Triple K;

The Brands Quilt

FIGURE 2
The Brands Quilt (detail)

FIGURE 3
The Brands Quilt (detail)

geometric symbols, such as the Double Bar and the Double Rail, the Half Box, the Rafter, and the Open A; and pictorial symbols, such as the Hay Hook, the Timbling Ladder, the Spur, and the Stirrup. The cowboy learned to read them in the correct order from left to right, from top to bottom, or from outside to inside. His acquired proficiency would lead Evans Coleman, an Arizona cowpuncher, to remark that a good cowboy could understand "the Constitution of the United States were it written with a branding iron on the side of a cow."[3]

NOTES

1. William H. Forbis, *The Cowboys* (New York: Time-Life Books, 1973), p. 133.

2. *The Stock Manual* (Forth Worth, Tex.: George B. Loving, 1881). The publication of the book was additionally supported by stock-related advertisements; on page 85, for example, utilizing a large woodblock of a rather elegant stagecoach, the Dodge City and Pan-Handle and U. S. Mail Line presented itself as the "Only stage running between Dodge City and the Pan-Handle. Leaving Dodge City at 7 p.m. via Camp Supply, Indian Territory, to Fort Elliott, Texas, making close connection with the Atchison, Topeka and Santa Fe Railroad at Dodge City."

3. Forbis, *The Cowboys*, p. 133.

PART 7

"The Wagon, a Blue Hen, and Forty Dollars"

FOR CALIFORNIA'S QUILTS and their makers, the transition from the late nineteenth century to the early twentieth was a seamless one. Women continued to make quilts to cover their sleeping children, to present to a minister off to tend to another flock, to record the names of families and friends, to raise funds for all manner of community causes—or for the pure pleasure of setting needle and thread to cloth. Cotton continued to be the principal fabric of choice, although the colors would change with the fashions, as they had done in the past. Deep indigos and rich tobacco browns comprised the palette of the past; now it was primarily pastels that filled the quilt-maker's sewing basket.

And still there were quilts that were California bound. Although the adventurers and the argonauts and a generation of their descendants had populated the state, by the 1930s the "migrations" had begun again. For one group, the migration was one of desperation. These were the victims of the Depression and the Dust Bowl. In March 1936, Dorothea Lange, the extraordinary photographic chronicler of those newly migrant workers, drove down a muddy lane into a pea-pickers camp in Nipomo, California, where she shot five exposures of a woman and her children—a sleeping baby and two tousle-haired young girls who hid their faces on their mother's shoulders. The woman looked away, her hand to her face. It was an image of ragged resignation, and it became an American icon. "She said that they had been living on frozen vegetables from the surrounding fields and birds that the children killed,"[1] Lange wrote. Years later, the woman in that photograph, Florence Thompson, recalled:

> when Steinbeck wrote in *The Grapes of Wrath* about those people living under the bridge in Bakersfield—at one time we lived under that bridge. It was the same story. Didn't even have a tent then, just a ratty old quilt.[2]

A second group, retirees from the rest of the country, particularly from the heartland, set aside their snow shovels and set off for the land of palm trees and oranges. Like the earlier travelers, they brought quilts with them: quilts of the century past that had traveled to the Midwest and no further and quilts that the new travelers themselves had worked in that unbroken tradition that now stretched across the continent.

These were the new Californians. Like the men and women before them, they found new homes, where new lives could be led, and where new quilts could be made.

NOTES

1. Dorothea Lange, field notes, quoted in Rebecca Maksel, "Migrant Madonna," *Smithsonian* (March 2002): 22.
2. Ibid.

THE BIGGS METHODIST EPISCOPAL QUILT

Biggs, Butte County, California, marked 1897
Made by the Ladies Aid Society
Cotton; pieced, embroidered, and quilted
79 x 77 in. (200.7 x 195.6 cm)
Collection of the Harkness family

FOR FAMILIES MOVING WEST, the Oregon Trail was the earlier and the easier of the routes to the Pacific Ocean, and it was from that territory that settlers might eventually move yet again, now south into California. A "forty-niner" near Sutterville encountered

> a family that had been wandering about since 1845 without having entered a house. There were two men, a woman, and three children. They started from one of the Eastern states with a wagon, two yoke of oxen, and two cows, passed through Missouri, crossed the Rocky Mountains into Oregon, and finally drove down to California. The children were all natives of the forest except the eldest. They were encamped under a large oak-tree a short distance from the river. The bed was made up on the ground, the sheets of snowy whiteness. The kitchen furniture was well arranged against the root of the tree. The children were building a playhouse of sticks, while the Mother was sitting in a "Boston rocker" reading the Bible, with a Methodist hymn-book in her lap.[1]

This is the way Methodism came to California, through Methodist hymnals and Methodist hearts.

It was circuit riders that often brought an irregular religious presence to the small town of Biggs.[2] Church services were held in the waiting room of the depot, then in C. S. Quimby's butcher shop, and later in the hall above the Buffington and Smith store. A Baptist church was built in 1874, and Methodist services were held there one Sunday each month. The Biggs Methodist Episcopal Church was truly begun with the laying of a cornerstone on Thanksgiving Day, November 24, 1887. Miss Celia Lewis sang "The Church in the Wildwood" and the ladies of the church served a Thanksgiving dinner to the public in Hamilton Hall.

In 1876, the Ladies Union in Biggs seems to have set a high standard for women's philanthropic efforts in Butte County, raising money by serving oyster suppers, presenting tableaux, and holding rabbit shoots. The organization was not affiliated with any particular church, although a local pastor had urged the ladies to organize themselves "into sewing societies for the support of the gospel."[3]

Like its predecessor, the Ladies Aid Society of 1887 was considered a secular organization, but it headed the subscription list for the building of the new Methodist church. It pledged, and immediately paid, $300 and subsequently made additional expenditures for sofa and chairs ($29.00), carpets ($116.90), seats and settee ($649.73), organ ($175.00), and freight and

The Biggs Methodist Episcopal Quilt

expenses ($114.95) for a total of $1,385.58. The society officially affiliated with the church in 1900, making an additional contribution of $125.00 at the dedication services.[4]

In the closing decades of the nineteenth century, when funds were particularly required for a church's coffers, ladies aid societies in substantial numbers stepped up to the task, most often armed with needles and thread. The numerous extant examples of signature-laden fund-raising quilts suggest overwhelmingly that this was a strong Methodist tradition, and that red embroidery on a white ground was the most popular medium.

The organization and execution of the Biggs quilt probably followed what seems to have been a rather standard procedure. The project would proceed in stages, utilizing a variety of the members' particular personal and technical skills. First, a committee would decide upon the overall design. In this instance, a particularly ambitious format was selected: each of twenty-five blocks would be pieced in a pattern classically referred to as "Wild Goose Chase" (FIG. 1). Then the blocks were distributed to ladies who set out to secure signatures and monies; in exchange for a modest sum (usually about twenty-five cents), the generous donor could sign the block or have his or her name written on the quilt by the persuasive solicitor.

Next, unless the names had been written in indelible ink, the blocks would be passed on (as in the Biggs quilt) to another group who embroidered

over the penciled signatures, almost always with Turkey red cotton floss. Additional hands took over the task of assembling the blocks and then—on to the quilting frame!

The quilt was usually auctioned off at some celebratory event, with those final funds swelling the proceeds. Several of these quilts seem to have ended up in the hands of the project's director, probably the result of a proud husband outbidding all others to return his wife's triumph to her grateful hands.

And this quilt was a triumph indeed, both aesthetically and financially: close to 950 names—some from the surrounding area—are inscribed on its vibrant surface. This large number, from such a small town, is a tribute to the persistence (and probably the social prominence) of those involved.[5]

Emma Amelia Walker was president of the Ladies Aid Society when this quilt was worked, and as the quilt has descended in her family it seems reasonable to think that its creation was her vision. Although she and her friends would not have known it at the time, they were constructing a historically significant community document: the town's most prominent citizens and pioneers are represented on the quilt, including, of course, Emma's husband, William Ashley Walker (1843–1912), the town's mayor and a major contractor in the Biggs-Gridley area, who supervised the church's construction and donated the bricks for its foundation and walls. Mr. Walker began his career as a brick manufacturer in 1861; he furnished the brick for the Butte County courthouse, infirmary, and county jail and built nearly all of the business blocks and houses in Biggs. Born on a farm in St. Francis County, Missouri, in 1843, he and his family crossed the Isthmus of Panama, arriving in San Francisco on November 21, 1856. Settling in Biggs by 1871, he married Louisa Nancy, whose parents, Thomas R. and Amanda Sligar, came to California by wagon train from Tennessee in the late 1850s. Having born two children, Louisa died, and as was often the case, William (in 1890) married her younger sister, Emma Amelia (FIG. 2), and she had a daughter of her own. The center block of the quilt (FIG. 3) records this family's history; the quilt records the community's.

FIGURE 3
The Biggs Methodist Episcopal Quilt
(detail)

NOTES

1. *A Pictorial View of California: Including a Description of the Panama and Nicaragua Routes* (New York: Henry Bill, 1853), p. 60.

2. One of these circuit riders, originally preaching in Biggs, Hamilton, Nelson, Gridley, and Live Oak, was Reverend E. Hopkins, who walked rather than rode. In 1885 he reported that he had walked over one thousand miles, "that the congregations were good, and that his health for which he had come to California was poor"; see Arthur D. Osborn, *A History of the Biggs, Butte County Area*, unpublished thesis, 1953, p. 84.

3. Quoted in *Biggs United Methodist Church Centennial Directory 1874–1974* (Biggs, Calif.: n.d.), pp. 31–32.

4. Ibid., p. 32.

5. Other towns mentioned on the quilt include: Chico, Fresno, Gridley, Kalamazoo, Lakeview, Oroville, San Francisco, San Rafael, Thermalito, and Tulare.

THE VINCENT METHODIST EPISCOPAL BEDCOVER

Los Angeles, California, marked 1904
Made by the V.M.E.C. Building Fund Group
Cotton; embroidered
85 x 82 in. (215.9 x 208.3 cm)
Private collection

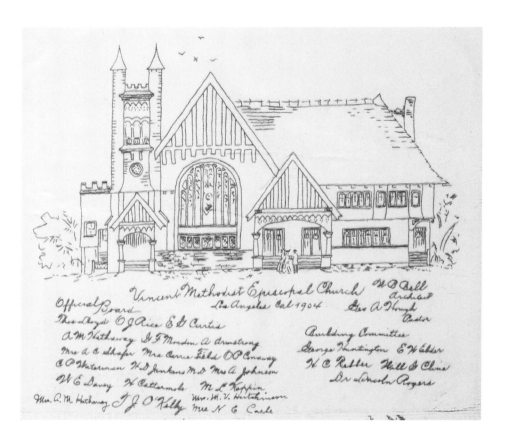

FIGURE 1
The Vincent Methodist Episcopal Bedcover
(detail)

IN ADDITION TO BRIEFLY NOTING special church-related events ("Reverend and Mrs. St. John are holding temperance evangelistic services at Temperance Temple every Sabbath afternoon at 3 o'clock") and providing items of personal interest ("Presiding Elder Caswell and wife have both been down with an attack of grip this week"), the "Methodist News" column in the *California Independent* also noted the success of two fund-raising activities:

> Boyle Heights Ladies Aid Society recently realized $37 for the parsonage fund.

> Ontario Church ladies gave an Art Exhibit at Odd Fellows Hall, on Friday evening of this week. It was a collection of rare treasures and netted its fair promoters a handsome profit. Refreshments were served.[1]

Elsewhere on the same page, a longer article reported on the Vincent Methodist Episcopal Church in Los Angeles. Although the reporter praised the "good revival work going on there for about a month" with its popular pastor, Rev. W. R. Knighten, leading "the forces to victory," he noted that "It is not

The Vincent Methodist Episcopal Bedcover

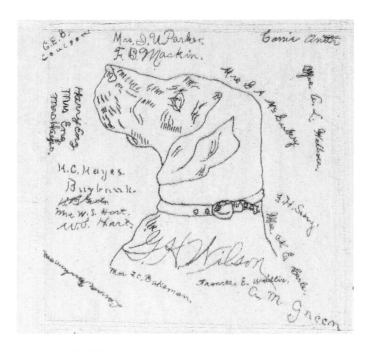

FIGURE 2
The Vincent Methodist Episcopal Bedcover
(detail)

FIGURE 3
The Vincent Methodist Episcopal Bedcover
(detail)

the handsomest church in the world on the outside. ..." In this critical obser-
vation, the congregation seems to have heard a clarion call and, perhaps moved
to action, shortly thereafter formed a Building Fund Committee.

As did the ladies in Biggs, the feminine faithful in Los Angeles rose to
this new financial challenge, here with the working of an embroidered fund-
raiser.[2] Red and white were their colors of choice as well. Collected signatures
were scripted in very distinctive arrangements around and between embroidered motifs worked in the outline stitch, a new application of art to embroidery that found great popularity beginning in the 1860s. The technique,
simple and swift, was described rather grandly in *Harper's Bazar*:

> As the chief beauty of outline work depends upon grace and fidelity to form, it is
> naturally a craft demanding poetic instinct as well as delicate manipulation. In
> nothing else wrought with a needle does the worker achieve results so delightfully
> prompt.[3]

The central image is an architectural rendering, all spires and stained
glass windows, of "Vincent Methodist Episcopal Church / 1904" (see FIG. 1).
The architect is identified (W B Bell), as is the new pastor (Geo A Hough).
The nineteen members of the Official Board are listed, as are the five members
of the Building Committee, and on the thirty-two blocks that surround this
central panel, over six hundred embroidered names attest to the generosity of
the congregation and the community.

Almost all the redwork motifs appear to have been worked from stamp-
ing, transfer, or perforated patterns. They were advertised primarily to be
applied to the small miscellaneous household linens being worked in seemingly
endless abundance: tea towels, table mats and tidies; doilies and pillow shams;
lambrequins, spoon holders, and splashers.[4]

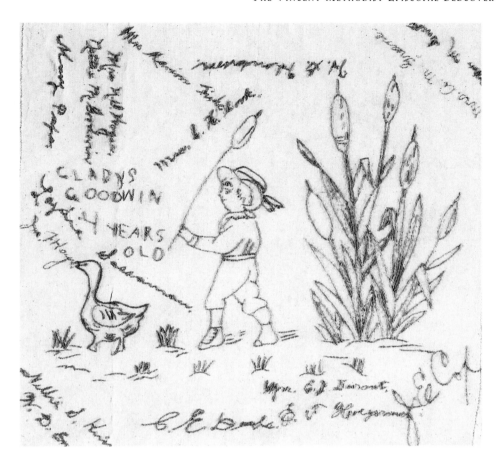

FIGURE 4
The Vincent Methodist Episcopal Bedcover
(detail)

The familiar dog's head (FIG. 2) and that of the dear little Puss (FIG. 3) appear often on redwork quilts, but the most popular designs for outline work were the precious children inspired by the line drawings and watercolors of the British illustrator Kate Greenaway. Many of them carry a long-stemmed flower; a sailor-suited little boy walking with a duck carries a cattail he has just plucked from a cluster behind him (FIG. 4). Contributors to a fund-raising quilt often made a contribution in the name of a child: appropriate to the youthful subject of this block is the name of "Gladys Goodwin / 4 years old."

NOTES

1. "Methodist News," *California Independent*, February 5, 1898.
2. Technically, the piece is a bedcover rather than a quilt. Machine-quilted lines run parallel to the seams, but they serve only to hold the front to the back. There is no batting present, or any quilting stitches.
3. *Harper's Bazar*, March 21, 1868, p. 324.
4. Numerous examples and period advertisements can be found in Deborah Harding, *Red & White: American Redwork Quilts* (New York: Rizzoli, 2000).

THE WORLD WAR I COMFORTER

Los Angeles, California, marked 1918
Maker unknown
Cotton; pieced and tied; inked inscriptions
75 x 60 in. (190.5 x 152.4 cm)
Los Angeles County Museum of Art;
gift of Sarah T. Kroger

IN ADDITION TO THE GIVING OVER OF SONS AND HUSBANDS, California women supported the First World War with a number of charitable undertakings. This red, white, and blue tied comforter was the result of a fund-raising project for the Government Aid Auxiliary.[1]

It is possible that many of the names were secured during a single, large social or patriotic function, with perhaps a strong Canadian association; among the numerous military signators (FIG. 1), many are identified as Canadian ("10th Canadian Engineers," "29th Battalion Canadians," etc.) and three are members of the Eaton family of Eaton's of Canada department store.

Among the well-known Los Angeles–area business, professional, and political men and women who contributed and inscribed their names were Edward Carter (a socially prominent department store owner), Harry Halde-

FIGURE I
The World War I Comforter (detail)

man (a well-to-do car dealer), "Bill" Evans (whose family owned a large plant nursery in Brentwood), and Nat Goodwin (an attorney who owned a nightclub in Santa Monica). Los Angeles Judge Joseph Scott contributed, as did former Senator John D. Works and Alyce Rogers, secretary of the National Defense League.[2]

It is in the creative fields, however, that the signatures are the most fascinating and familiar. The surface of the comforter is an autograph book signed by contributing members of the fledgling film industry. Among the actors and actresses are Mary Pickford, Roscoe "Fatty" Arbuckle, Theda Bara, Charles Ray, Lewis J. Cody, and Mabel Moore. The director Wm. D. Taylor (an early movie director later murdered in one of Hollywood's most sensational murder cases) is included, as is Frances Marion, a scenario writer for the early movies. The stage is represented by Sarah Bernhardt and Walter Hampden (the great, early Shakespearean actor), and by Fred Stone (an early vaudeville performer) and Leon Erroll (an early stage and movie comedian). Composers Charles Wakefield Cadman and Homer Grunn penned several bars of their compositions.

Most interesting of all, the surface is illustrated with numerous political cartoons. One, unsigned, is a pensive portrait of Miss Liberty (FIG. 2). A popular political symbol since the early days of the republic, she enjoyed a particular vogue as a cartoon figure beginning in the late nineteenth century; here,

The World War I Comforter

FIGURE 2
The World War I Comforter (detail)

FIGURE 3
The World War I Comforter (detail)

traditionally, she wears a star-spangled Liberty Cap.[3] Another cartoon shows a dazed German officer, a tilted helmet worn atop his clumsily bandaged head; it is signed by "Major J. A. Osborne / Canadian Expeditionary Force / 1918" (FIG. 3).

One block (FIG. 4) contains five cartoons drawn by some of the leading cartoonists of the period: in the center, firmly clenching his cigar, flower in his lapel, is *Jiggs*, drawn and signed by G. McManus; top left is the contribution of F. Opper, the famous creator of *Happy Hooligan*, *Maud*, and *Alphonse and Gaston*; top right are the jolly Hans and Fritz, *The Katzenjammer Kids*, drawn by Harold Knorr; bottom right, the Kaiser has been unceremoniously dumped in the Ash Can, "His Future Throne," by Rube Goldberg; and bottom left, C. R. Macauley, "Oct.23 – 1918," memorialized a somber "Uncle Sam"—less than a month later, the Kaiser had abdicated and an armistice had been signed.

Between celebrities, commerce, and cartoons, one might have failed to notice a particularly poignant inscription: someone made a contribution for, and signed on his behalf, "Richard Ward Bondy, Age 10 months / My daddy is in France."

FIGURE 4
The World War I Comforter (detail)

NOTES

1. Mrs. Walter R. (Sarah) Kroger, correspondence accompanying the object, 1938.

2. My investigation of this piece began in 1985; the late Satch LeValley was particularly helpful in identifying a number of the names, particularly in the Los Angeles area's business and social circles.

3. The droopy cap (derived from classical times, when it was worn by freed slaves) was often carried in political parades on top of Liberty Poles, symbols of the pine tree, or Liberty Tree, under which the Sons of Liberty (a secret, pre-Revolutionary society) gathered.

THE HOLLYWOOD BEDCOVER

Los Angeles, California, ca. 1931
Maker unknown
Cotton; embroidered
86 x 73 in. (218.4 x 185.4 cm)
Private collection

ALTHOUGH NOT QUITE "A CAST OF THOUSANDS,"[1] the 205 figures and faces on this embroidered bedcover form a veritable cavalcade of celebrities, an important group portrait of Hollywood in its golden years. The movie fan that undertook this production left us no credit line bearing her name, and she set out no plot to explain the story of how or why it was worked. The only possible clue may lie in the block portraying the large "Pilgrimage Play" cross rising up quite magnificently out of an area of tiny, stylized buildings including the Hollywood Bowl (FIG. 1). A wooden, outdoor amphitheater was built in the Cahuenga Pass in 1920 as the site of the religious performance; the play was performed by noted actors every summer until the original structure was destroyed by a brush fire that swept through the Pass in October 1929.

The names on this unquilted piece have been transcribed as "printed," except that the numerous letters such as "N," which were reversed, have been set right. Misspellings are rampant! The maker's obvious enthusiasm for the

FIGURE I
The Hollywood Bedcover (detail)

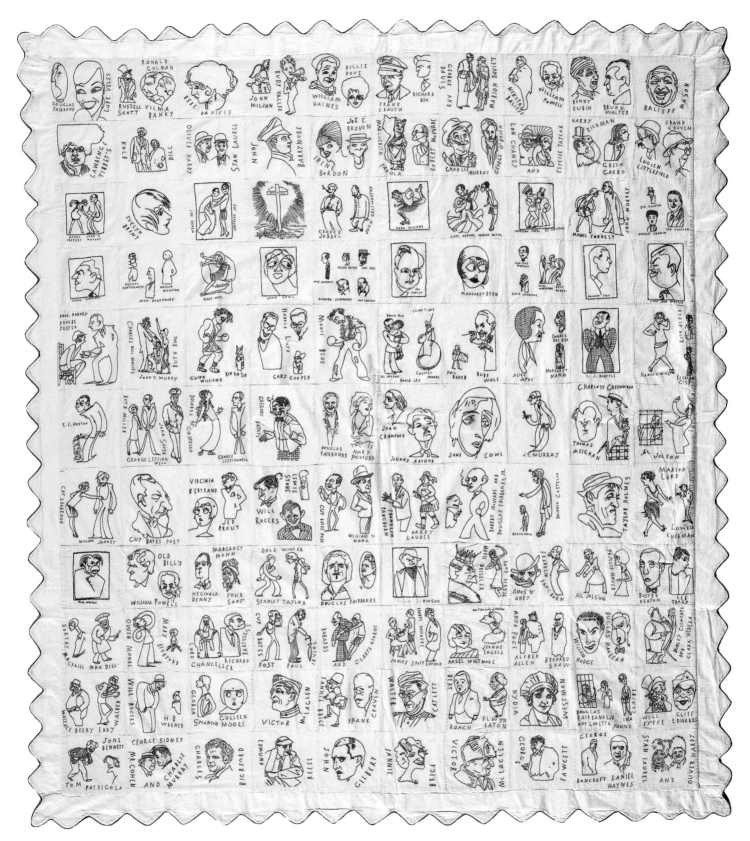

The Hollywood Bedcover

FIGURE 2
The Hollywood Bedcover (detail)

task at hand was not matched by any particular technical skill other than the ability to execute rather mediocre outline and straight embroidery stitches. One block, that of Edward G. Robinson (FIG. 2), may have served as a prototype in deciding how best to execute the names and faces: the first name and the first two letters of the last were worked in a thin, white thread over a clearly visible pencil line. From that point on, only blue cotton embroidery floss was used on the face and names throughout the work.

The numerous sources that provided the patterns for the figures are pure Hollywood! Probably 90 percent are identifiable from 1928–30 films, many from the 1926–27 classics of the early "talkies," including Monte Blue in *White Shadows in the South Seas* (FIGS. 3 and 4), Bebe Daniels in a still from *Rio Rita*, Daniel Hayne in *Hallelujah*, Lawrence Tibbett and Laurel and Hardy in their fur-hatted costumes from *The Rogue Song*. Most, such as two of the several images of Douglas Fairbanks (FIG. 5), are taken directly from photo movie stills (FIG. 6) or poster art (FIG. 7). Many appeared in exhibitors' campaign books, lavish productions printed a year in advance to promote the studio's forthcoming productions; others were printed in press books from which theaters could order posters, cardboard "standees" for the lobby, and other promotional material. The fan could have been working from movie magazines such as *Photoplay*. Caricatures, perhaps from *Vanity Fair* magazine, have been incorporated as well, identifiable from those faces taken from photographic

stills by their cleaner, clearer lines; Buster Keaton, for example (FIG. 8), was probably drawn by "Hap" Hadley, who did artwork for the studios and produced numerous caricatures of Keaton.[2]

This is obviously the work of a star-struck fan whose initial inspiration may have been nothing more than an 8 x 10-inch black-and-white publicity still of an incredibly handsome Gary Cooper (FIGS. 9 and 10).

FIGURE 3, ABOVE LEFT
The Hollywood Bedcover (detail)

FIGURE 4, ABOVE RIGHT
Monte Blue, in *White Shadows in the South Seas*, photograph (MGM, 1928)
Courtesy of the Academy of Motion Picture Arts and Sciences

FIGURE 5
The Hollywood Bedcover (detail)

FIGURE 6
Douglas Fairbanks in *The Iron Mask*, photograph (United Artists, 1929)
Courtesy of the Academy of Motion Picture Arts and Sciences

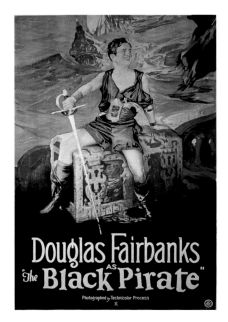

FIGURE 7
Douglas Fairbanks in *The Black Pirate*, poster (United Artists, 1926) *Courtesy of the Academy of Motion Picture Arts and Sciences*

FIGURE 8
The Hollywood Bedcover (detail)

FIGURE 9, LEFT
The Hollywood Bedcover (detail)

FIGURE 10, ABOVE
Gary Cooper in *The Winning of Barbara Worth*, photograph (United Artists, 1926) *Courtesy of the Academy of Motion Picture Arts and Sciences*

NOTES

1. Eighteen celebrities—including John Barrymore, Fanny Brice, Dolores Costello, Colleen Moore, Mary Pickford, William Powell, and Will Rogers—appear more than once, in different roles. Their names rampantly misspelled, the "cast of thousands"* are:

1a. Douglas Fairbank / Lupe Velez
1b. Russell Scott / Ronald Colman / Vilma Banky
1c. Bebe Daniels
1d. John Miljan / Rudy Vallee
1e. William Haines / Billie Dove
1f. Frank Craven / Richard Dix
1g. George and Davis / Marion Davie's
1h. Nikita Balieff / William Powell
1i. Benny Rubin / Bruno Walter
1j. Balieff Mason
2a. Lawrence Tibbet's
2b. Kolb / Dill
2c. Oliver Hardy / Stan Laurel
2d. John Barrymore
2e. Irene Bordon / Joe E. Brown
2f. Marguerita Padula / Robert McWade
2g. Charlie Murray / George O'Brien
2h. Lon Chaney and Estelle Taylor
2i. Harry Richman / Greta Garbo
2j. Lucien Littlefield / Frank Craven
3a. Mabel Forrest / John T. Murray
3b. Evelyn Brent
3c. Joe Pepew / Jeatrice Joy
3d. In Hoc / (illegible) inzes / The Pilgrimage Play / Art, Music / Literature / The Bowl / Hollywood
3e. George Jessel / John Galsworthy
3f. Vera Villiers
3g. Carl Gerard / Norma Drew
3h. Harrison Ford / El Capital
3i. Marel Forrest / John Murray
3j. Syd Chaplin / Charlie Chaplin / Syd Chaplin
4a. George Sherwood
4b. Richard Barthelmess / John Barrymore / Marcia Mannimg
4c. Peggy Hope
4d. Jane Cowl
4e. Jack Mulhull / Helen Hayes / Chic Sale / Rudolph Schildkraut / Gus Edwards
4f. Leo Carillo
4g. Margaret Been
4h. Adolphe Menjou / Emile Jannings / Mabel Whitmore / Bela Habosi
4i. Harrison Ford
4j. Louis John Bartels
5a. Paul Harvey / Phoebe Foster
5b. Charles Hill Malles / John T. Murry / Ruth King
5c. Guinn Williams / Rin Tin Tin
5d. Harold Loyd / Gary Cooper
5e. Monte Blue
5f. Al Jolson / Sonny Boy / Lilac Time / Colleen Moore / David Lee
5g. Phil Baker / Rube Wole
5h. Alice Joyce / Dolores Del Reo / Margaret Mann
5i. L. J. Bartels
5j. Nance O'Neil's / Ruth Alder / Lillian Cist
6a. E. E. Horton
6b. Ruth Miller / John Sousa / George Leffingwell
6c. Dolores Costello / George Leffingwell
6d. Gregory Ratoff
6e. Douglas Fairbanks / Mary Pickford
6f. Joan Crawford / Johnny Arthur
6g. Jane Cowl
6h. J. T. Murray
6i. Charlotte Greenwood / Thomas Meighan
6j. Al Jolson
7a. Gay Seabrook / William Janney
7b. Guy Bates Post
7c. Virginia Bertrand / Jed Rrout
7d. Will Rogers / Lewis Stone
7e. Guy Bates Post / William V. Mong
7f. Franklin Pancborn / Harry Lauder
7g. Robert McWade and Douglas Fairbanks Jr.
7h. Baclanova / Dolores Costello
7i. Taylor Holmes
7j. Marion Lord / Lowell Sherman
8a. Paul Wedner
8b. Old Bill's / William Powell
8c. Heginald Denny / Margaret Mann / Four Sons
8d. Dale Winter / Stanley Taylor
8e. Douglas Fairbanks
8f. Edward Robinson
8g. Marie Dressler / Bessie Love
8h. Amos 'n Andy / Franklin Pancborn
8i. Al Jolson / Phyllis Haver
8j. Buster Keaton / Lee Tracy
9a. Dortav Mackaill / Max Dill
9b. Owen Moore / Mary Pickford
9c. Lord Chanceller / Richard Barteless
9d. Guy Bates Post / Paul Irving
9e. Robards and Gladys George
9f. Isabel Withers / James Spotswood
9g. Hazel Whitmore / Jeanne Eagels
9h. Anita Pace / Alfred Allen / Bernard Shaw
9i. William Hodge / Duglas MacLean
9j. Dudley Clements / Clara Vedera
10a. Wallace Beery / Eddy Walker
10b. Will Rogers / H. B. Warner
10c. Gloria Swanson / Colleec Moore
10d. Victor McLaglen
10e. Fannie Brice / Frank Craven
10f. Walter Catlett
10g. Bert Roach / Flwyn Eaton
10h. Nydia Westman
10i. Douglas Fairbanks, Jr. and Loretta Young / Ina Claire
10j. Will Fyffe / Cliff Edwards
11a. Tom Patricola / Jone Bennett
11b. Mr. Cohen and Charlie Murray / George Sidney
11c. Charles Bickford
11d. Edmund Reese
11e. John Gilbert
11f. Fannie Brice
11g. Victor McLaglen
11h. George Fawcett
11i. George Bancroft / Daniel Haynes
11j. Stan Laurel and Oliver Hardy

2. I am extremely grateful to Beth Werling, film historian and Collection Manager at the Natural History Museum of Los Angeles County, for her generous collaboration on this particular artifact. Her unerring identification of the sources of the images was critical to the text.

* Numbers refer to the rows that run top to bottom, and letters to those that run left to right. Block 1a, therefore, would be in the upper left-hand corner.

THE MOUNT WILSON OBSERVATORY QUILT

Probably Pasadena, California, ca. 1930
Maker unidentified
Cotton; appliquéd, embroidered, and quilted
82 x 65 in. (208.3 x 165.1 cm)
Private collection

IN 1864, BENJAMIN WILSON BUILT A TRAIL to the top of a wild mountain in Southern California's Sierra Madre range that rose a mile high above his
ranch. The lumber he had sought proved unsuitable for his purposes, and the
trail up what was to be called Wilson's Peak was abandoned.

Almost a decade later, in 1873, settlers from Indiana established the Indiana Colony on a segment of Wilson's old ranch. The community of Pasadena
thus established, and soon thriving, all activity focused there on the valley. Little wonder that the old trail received scant attention: when the great naturalist
John Muir climbed near the peak in 1877, he reported it to be "more rigidly
inaccessible than any other I ever attempted to penetrate."[1] But once it was
restored, the lure of the trail and of the mountain proved irresistible to the
hardier members of the small community. The nine miles remained a difficult
two-day trip on horseback or mule, but once reached, it was a grand view
indeed!

In the post–Civil War period, the study of astronomy was limited primarily to the measurement of the positions of the stars and their brightness and
motions, but there was a keen amateur interest. *The Girl's Home Companion*, a
late-nineteenth-century manual for young ladies, discussed and illustrated an
extensive number of indoor and outdoor "amusements"—from croquet to tat-
ting—and devoted fifteen pages to a decidedly poetic study of astronomy.

> The charm of a still, clear starlight night is felt, we believe, by everyone possessed
> of the least culture or taste; but the number at present is very few of those young
> girls who can call the brilliant orbs by their names, and look intelligently on the
> starry heavens. And yet no science is more sublime or captivating than Astron-
> omy; it appeals to our highest faculties; to our fancy and imagination.[2]

In 1889–90 on Wilson's Peak, looking out—and up—a group of Harvard
astronomers tested observing conditions on the mountain for the University of
Southern California, which had been promised funding toward the building of
the world's largest telescope. Everything seemed to be working against the
project: the effects of one of the most severe winters on record damaged the
instruments, the economy worsened, campers interfered with the procedures,
and so on. After eighteen months the site, like the trail, was adandoned.[3]

George Ellery Hale (one of the leading astronomers of the period) had not
yet been born when Benjamin Wilson laid his trail to the top of that rugged
mountain, but he stood on Wilson's Peak in 1903 and determined to build his
solar observatory on that spot. And this he did. With its great telescopes
installed, Mount Wilson Observatory dominated astronomy throughout the

The Mount Wilson Observatory Quilt

FIGURE I
The Mount Wilson Observatory Quilt
(detail)

first half of the twentieth century, and the discoveries made there—the nature of the galaxies, the composition of the stars, the workings of the sun, the structure of the universe—altered forever the way we look at the heavens.

From that point on, in Pasadena, on what had been Benjamin Wilson's ranch, interest in astronomy and in the activities on Mount Wilson ran at an occasionally fevered pitch, both communally and commercially. When George Hale signed a ninety-nine-year lease on the forty acres on which the observatory was to be built, it came to him rent free: the Mount Wilson Toll Road Company recognized the financial potential from international tourism. "The

Mount Wilson War" was waged to determine which entrepreneurial interests would prevail at the foot of the mountain. And there was the simple matter of community pride!

Yet, we can only imagine the inspiration for this celestial creation, the *Mount Wilson Observatory Quilt*. Two of the observatory's architectural elements, the dome of the 100-inch telescope (FIG. 1) and the 150-foot solar tower telescope[4] (FIG. 2), are appliquéd and embroidered and they are surrounded by the objects of its studies: the moon and Saturn are set among ninety-three scattered stars, eight of which form the Big Dipper. Hundreds of small, five-point stars form the quilted ground. In the Sears, Roebuck and Company building that was constructed for the 1933 Chicago World's Fair—known as the Century of Progress Exposition—the most popular exhibit featured the winners from among more than 24,000 entries in the national quilt competition the company had sponsored.[5] Thematically and technically, this would have been a competitive entry.

Worked for whatever reason, the quilt celebrates George Hale's great vision:

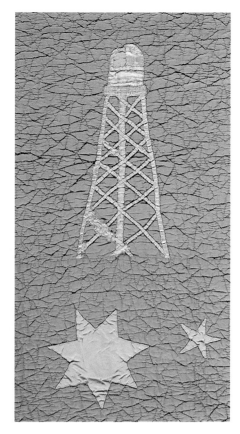

FIGURE 2
The Mount Wilson Observatory Quilt
(detail)

> *A picture growing clear before his eyes*
> *Of all that was to be in years to come*
> *Upon that mountaintop.*
> —Harold Babcock, "In 1903"[6]

NOTES

1. All factual elements regarding the observatory have been drawn, passim, from the exemplary works of Michael Simmons, who wrote a series of articles for The Mount Wilson Observatory Association—"Bringing Astronomy to an Isolated Mountaintop" (1983), "Entering a New Era in Solar Research" (1983), and "Building the 60-Inch Telescope" (1984)—and of W. S. Adams, who wrote an earlier article, "Early Solar Research at Mount Wilson" (1955), for the review journal *Vistas in Astronomy* (vol. 1, pp. 619–23).

2. Mrs. Valentine, ed., *The Girl's Companion: A Book of Pastimes in Work and Play* (London and New York: Frederick Warne and Co., n.d.), p. 577.

3. After the 13-inch refractor left the mountain in 1890, an observatory with a 16-inch refractor was built on nearby Echo Mountain by Professor Thaddeus Lowe. It continued to operate for another thirty-four years.

4. The dome on the top of the tower holds the optical instruments, including mirrors that follow the Sun throughout the day and the lens that forms the image of the Sun on the instruments at ground level. Michael Simmons, correspondence with the author, May 1, 2002.

5. "Sears National Quilt Contest, 1933," in Merikay Waldvogel, *Soft Covers for Hard Times: Quiltmaking & the Great Depression* (Nashville, Tenn.: Rutledge Hill Press, 1990), pp. 38–47.

6. Source unidentified.

THE "HAM AND EGGS" QUILT

Probably Los Angeles, California, marked 1939
Made by Eva Truxillo and Irene Brewster
Cotton; embroidered and tied
100 x 72 in. (254 x 182.9 cm)
Private collection

CALIFORNIA WAS WHERE ONE MOVED TO RETIRE. In the 1930s, the state was disproportionately elderly,[1] so it is not surprising that, during those years, pension schemes found an appreciative audience there.[2] Perhaps the most interesting of these was the Ham and Eggs California Pension Plan, originated by a Los Angeles radio commentator named Robert Noble. Simply put, the Ham and Eggs plan called for the state of California to pay $30 in "scrip," every Thursday, to each unemployed Californian fifty years of age or older.

The plan was of questionable economic merit (President Franklin Roosevelt called it an unwise "shortcut to Utopia"[3]) and unfortunately it was directed by men of questionable character. But it attracted 300,000 members (each paying dues of 30 cents per month), and was supported by many more, and in 1938 it actually propelled itself onto the ballot.

> Then one day—just three short weeks before the (1938) California primaries—the Pension Plan presented Frank C. Jordan, Secretary of State, with the largest list of petitions in the history of California: 789,000 voters—25% of the registration—were demanding a chance to vote for Ham and Eggs for California. California politicians sat up with a jerk. It wasn't possible! Over three quarters of a million voters. Who were these people?[4]

The initiative was narrowly defeated: 1,143,670 to 1,398,999. The movement regrouped, and the November 7, 1939, date on this tied bedcover suggests that Eva Truxillo and Irene Brewster worked this ambitious fund-raiser to help place the proposition on the ballot yet again. The central panel restated the vision: "Retirement. Warranty / $30 A Week / for life / Ham and Eggs / for / Everybody" (FIG. 1). The names of more than 850 contributors were embroidered in various bright colored threads (FIGS. 2 and 3); among them are a number of merchants, shops, and businesses, including the Ethelen Bell Rest Home.

The Ham and Eggs plan was defeated once more, and legal technicalities prevented it from appearing on subsequent ballots.

NOTES

1. It was not until World War II and the years thereafter that younger job seekers began to arrive in California in any substantial numbers.
2. The Social Security Act was enacted in 1935, but the system was not scheduled to pay out pensions until 1942. It was advanced to 1940 when the trust fund exceeded expectations.
3. Transcript, Presidential broadcast, August 15, 1938, Franklin D. Roosevelt Library.
4. Winston Moore and Marian Moore, *Out of the Frying Pan* (Los Angeles: DeVorss & Co., 1939), p. 77, quoted in Daniel J. B. Mitchell, "The Lessons of Ham and Eggs: California's 1938 and 1939 Pension Ballot Propositions," *Historical Society of Southern California, Southern California Quarterly* 82, no. 2 (Summer 2000): 193.

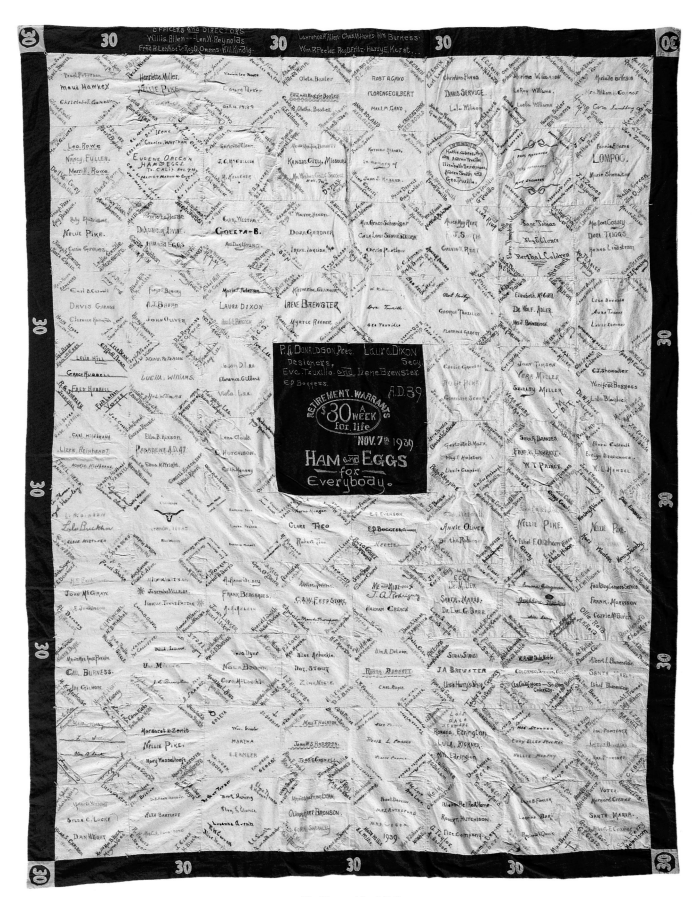

The "Ham and Eggs" Quilt

FIGURE 1
The "Ham and Eggs" Quilt (detail)

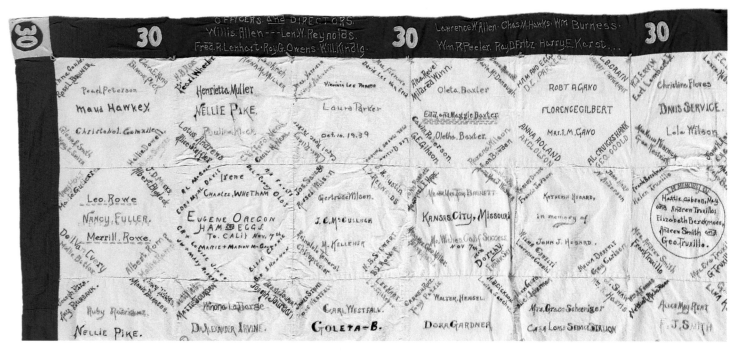

FIGURE 2
The "Ham and Eggs" Quilt (detail)

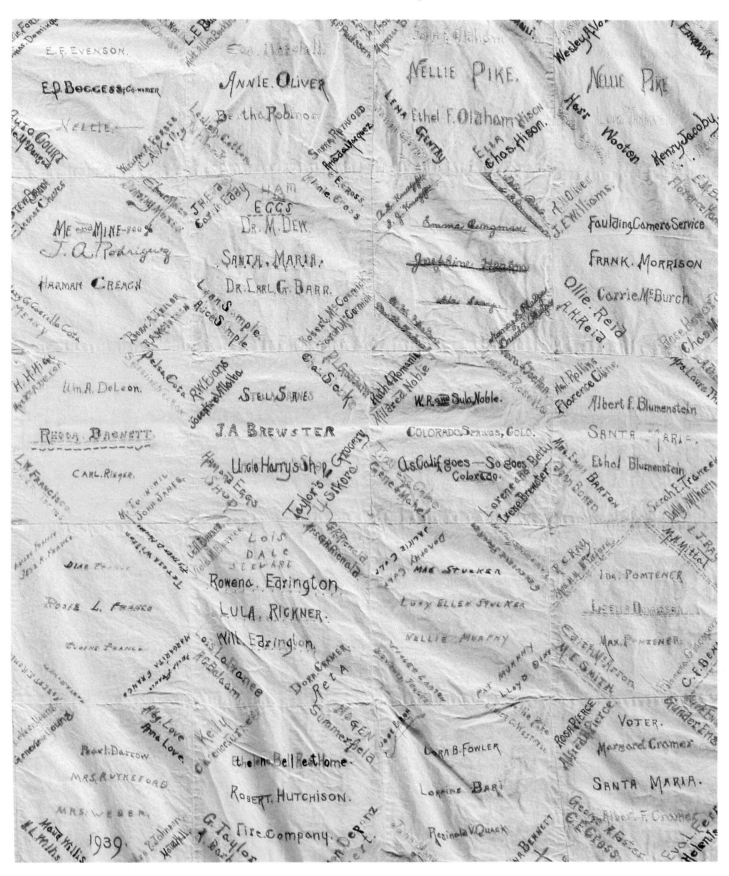

FIGURE 3
The "Ham and Eggs" Quilt (detail)

THE LAGUNA BEACH QUILT

Laguna Beach, California, ca. 1940
Maker unknown
Cotton; pieced, appliquéd, and quilted
85 ½ x 73 ¼ in. (217.2 x 186.1 cm)
Los Angeles County Museum of Art;
gift of Grace Powell Narver

THIS PASTEL, COTTON QUILT has captured the serene character of the community in which it was worked, Laguna Beach, California, ca. 1940. The hard lines of the classic "log cabin" quilt have given way to a new dwelling: the soft, sweeping roof of a cozy bungalow that nestles just behind a rolling hill on a cliff dropping off to the sea below beneath a blue, cloud-filled sky (FIG. 1). It is a scene of the contentment that the pioneers must have envisioned a century earlier.

The beginnings of this California community were similar to so many others. In November 1871, George and Sarah Thurston, with six of their eventual thirteen children, drove a wagon into Aliso Canyon and settled on the briefly held and now-abandoned claim (one of the earliest in the area) of Eugene Slater, who lived as a bachelor and could not abide the isolation. The dwelling they found was a one-room sheep camp, only 12 x 14 feet, without doors but with plenty of snakes.

FIGURE 1
The Laguna Beach Quilt (detail)

The Laguna Beach Quilt

FIGURE 2
The Laguna Beach Quilt (detail)

NOTES

1. The Orange County Historical Society, *Orange County History Series* 2 (1932): 48.
2. Don Meadows, "Early Laguna Beach," in *The Historical Volume and Reference Works*, vol. 3 (Whittier, Calif.: Historical Publishers, 1963), p. 241.
3. In 1918, Esther Virginia Sharp wrote to her daughter, Virginia Tolerton:

    > About two or three weeks after you were born, the Tolerton's decided (they always decided everything for me) that I should go to Laguna with you for the summer, as it was so hot in Pasadena....I had to stay there [in May's house] alone with a tiny baby ... and for blocks and blocks around there was only one other house.

    See Roger W. Jones, *California from the Conquistadores to the Legends of Laguna* (Laguna Beach, Calif.: Rockledge Enterprises, 1997), p. 379.
4. Ibid., pp. 372–73.
5. The initials are cut from transfer patterns in a style that more usually would have been worked on towels or pillowcases.

In front of this shack these pioneers at once placed a tent. They had brought pieces of wood sufficient for flooring. Later they built a room in front of the tent and several years afterward a barn, bringing the lumber from Newport. ... The other possessions of the family consisted of the team of ponies, the wagon, a blue hen, and forty dollars.[1]

Dressed in gunnysack aprons, George and Sarah and the oldest of the children cleared the rough field. They somehow prospered.

Although bordered on the north by Rancho San Joaquin (granted by the Mexican governor Juan Alvarado to Jose Sepulveda), much of the land south to the ocean had never been part of a Mexican or Spanish grant and was therefore government land. Most was too unsuitable for cultivation, but it was available to homesteaders through the Timber-Culture Act of 1871. They eventually came, to claim their 160 acres of land and to begin to plant the required ten acres of trees. In Laguna, these were invariably the Australian eucalyptus; those 1880s groves established the visual character of the area. And what a spectacular area it was! The natural canyon passed through the hills to a shallow lagoon near its head; when the Spanish discovered it, they called it *Canyada de Laguna* (the Canyon of the Lagoon).[2] The flat basin quickly rose to steep cliffs, with more than thirty individual coves and beaches along eight and a half miles of the Pacific Ocean.

Laguna's topography, and eventually the inclinations of its citizens, precluded its development in agriculture or manufacturing. It became, instead, a vacationing spot for Southern Californians wishing to escape the inland heat[3] and, eventually, a flourishing art colony.

Amidst the eucalyptus trees and on the cliffs were Laguna's cottages—many of them owned by fruit growers from Corona and Riverside—awaiting the summer migrations. Wilbur Douglas Tolerton recalled that as a young man, around 1909, he would ride his bicycle down Laguna Canyon to visit his sister's beach house:

> There were not many cottages in Laguna. ... We walked around at night with lanterns and knew everyone including the dogs and cats.[4]

Suggesting a continuing commemoration of those friendships formed are the initialed, heraldic-like devices[5] that surround the central image of the *Laguna Beach Quilt* (FIG. 2). They represent neighbors, perhaps, from summer days long ago in cottages perched at the edge of the cliff in that sleepy village (FIG. 3).

Those were California's halcyon days, appropriately reflected on one of California's quilts.

FIGURE 3
The twin bungalows of the Jahraus (left)
and the Skidmore families, Laguna
Beach, California, undated photograph
*Collection of Wells Fargo Bank, Laguna
Beach, photograph courtesy of Roger W.
Jones*

Bibliography

A Pictorial View of California: Including a Description of the Panama and Nicaragua Routes. New York: Henry Bill, 1853.

ADAMS, RAMON F. *Western Words: A Dictionary of the American West.* Norman: University of Oklahoma Press, 1968.

ADAMS, W. S. "Early Solar Research at Mount Wilson." *Vistas in Astronomy* 1 (1955): 619–23.

ALDRICH, MRS. THOMAS BAILEY. *Crowding Memories.* London: Constable, 1921.

ANDRIST, RALPH F., ed. *American Heritage History of the Making of a Nation.* New York: American Heritage Publishing Co., Inc., 1968.

BAKER, HUGH S. "Rational Amusements in Our Midst: Public Libraries in California, 1849–1859." *California Historical Society Quarterly* 38 (1959): 295–32.

BANCROFT, HUBERT HOWE. *History of California.* Vol. 6. San Francisco: The History Company, 1886.

Bespangled, Painted & Embroidered: Decorated Masonic Aprons in America 1790–1850. Exhibition Catalogue. Lexington, Mass.: Scottish Rite Masonic Museum of Our National Heritage, 1980.

Better Choose Me. Exhibition Brochure. North Newton, Kans.: Kaufman Museum, 1999.

BIDWELL, JOHN. "Life in California Before the Gold Discovery." *The Century Magazine* 61, no. 2 (December 1890): 163–83.

Biggs United Methodist Church Centennial Directory 1874–1974. Biggs, Calif.: n.d.

BLEVINS, WINFRED. *Dictionary of the American West.* New York: Facts on File, 1993.

BLUM, DILYS, AND JACK L. LINDSEY. "Nineteenth-Century Appliqué Quilts." Exhibition Catalogue. *Philadelphia Museum of Art Bulletin* 85, nos. 363, 364 (Fall 1989).

BRACKMAN, BARBARA. *Encyclopedia of Pieced Quilt Patterns.* Paducah, Ky.: American Quilter's Society, 1993.

BRANNAN, SAM. *The Messenger.* December 15, 1845.

BURR, WESLEY R., AND RUTH J. BURR. *A History of the Burr Pioneers.* Provo, Utah: The Charles and Sarah Burr Family Organization, 1995.

BUTTERFIELD, ROGER. *The American Past.* New York: Simon and Schuster, 1976.

California Pioneer Register and Index. Baltimore, Md.: Regional Publishing Co., 1964.

"California Statehood: New Economies and Opportunities." In *California History Guide.* Los Angeles: Natural History Museum of Los Angeles County, 2001.

CARPENTER, BENJAMIN. "Ben Carpenter's Sayings and Doings." 1849–1850. Unpublished manuscript. Los Angeles: Autry Museum of Western Heritage.

CARRUTH, JANET, AND LAURENE SINEMA. "Emma M. Andres and Her Six Grand Old Characters," *Uncoverings* (1990): 88–108.

CLEAVELAND, AGNES MORLEY. *No Life for a Lady.* Lincoln: University of Nebraska Press, 1977.

COLLINS, HERBERT RIDGEWAY. *Threads of History: America Recorded on Cloth 1775 to the Present.* Washington, D.C.: Smithsonian Institution Press, 1979.

CREWS, PATRICIA COX, ed. *A Flowering of Quilts.* Lincoln and London: University of Nebraska Press, 2001.

CREWS, PATRICIA COX, AND RONALD C. NAUGLE, eds. *Nebraska Quilts and Quiltmakers.* Lincoln and London: University of Nebraska Press, 1991.

DAKIN, SUSANNA BRYANT. *Rose or Rose Thorn? Three Women of California.* Berkeley: The Friends of the Bancroft Library, University of California, 1963.

DANA, RICHARD HENRY JR. *Two Years Before the Mast: A Personal Narrative of Life at Sea.* New York: The Heritage Press, 1947.

DAVIS, HON. WIN. J. *Illustrated History of Sacramento County, California.* Chicago: Lewis Publishing Company, 1890.

Davis, William Heath. *Seventy-Five Years in California.* San Francisco: John Howell, 1929.

De Tocqueville, Alexis. *Journey to America.* New Haven, Conn.: Yale University Press, 1960.

De Witt, Margaret. De Witt Family Papers. The Bancroft Library, University of California, Berkeley.

Dinan, John A. *The Pulp Western: A Popular History of the Western Fiction Magazine in America.* San Bernardino, Calif.: Borgo Press, 1983.

Driesbach, Janice T., Harvey L. Jones, and Katherine Church Holland. *Art of the Gold Rush.* Berkeley: Oakland Museum of California, Crocker Art Museum and University of California Press, 1998.

Dunton, William Rush Jr. *Old Quilts.* Catonsville, Md.: published by the author, 1946.

Englehardt, Fr. Zephyrin. *San Diego Mission.* San Francisco: James H. Barry Co., 1920.

Forbis, William H. *The Cowboys.* New York: Time-Life Books, 1973.

Ford, Janene. "Remnants of John Tam's Life and Career: Popular Entertainment and Medicine Shows, 1860–1896." *The Far-Westerner: The Quarterly Bulletin of the Stockton Corral of Westerners* 37, no. 3–4 (Fall/Winter, 1996): 5–39.

Fox, Sandi. *For Purpose and Pleasure: Quilting Together in Nineteenth-Century America.* Nashville, Tenn.: Rutledge Hill Press, 1995.

———. *Quilts in Utah: A Reflection of the Western Experience.* Salt Lake City, Utah: Salt Lake Art Center, 1981.

———. *Small Endearments: Nineteenth-Century Quilts for Children and Dolls.* Nashville, Tenn.: Rutledge Hill Press, 1994.

———. *Wrapped in Glory: Figurative Quilts & Bedcovers 1700–1900.* New York and London: Los Angeles County Museum of Art and Thames and Hudson, 1990.

Franco, Barbara. *Fraternally Yours: A Decade of Collecting.* Exhibition Catalogue. Lexington, Mass.: Scottish Rite Masonic Museum of Our National Heritage, 1986.

Fraternally Yours: A Decade of Collecting. Exhibition Catalogue. Lexington, Mass.: Scottish Rite Masonic Museum of Our National Heritage, 1986.

The Friend. Quaker publication, 1854.

Frye, Thomas, ed. *American Quilts: A Handmade Legacy.* Exhibition Catalogue. Oakland: Oakland Museum of California, 1981.

Garoutte, Sally. "California's First Quilting Party." *Uncoverings* (1981): 53–62.

George-Warren, Holly, and Michelle Freedman. *How the West Was Worn.* New York: Harry N. Abrams, Inc. in association with the Autry Museum of Western Heritage, Los Angeles, 2001.

Goldsborough, Jennifer Faulds. *Lavish Legacies: Baltimore Album and Related Quilts in the Collection of the Maryland Historical Society.* Baltimore: Maryland Historical Society, 1994.

Gregson, Eliza Marshall. "Mrs. Gregson's Memory." In "The Gregson Memoirs," *California Historical Quarterly* 19, no. 1 (1940): 113–43.

Gross, Joyce. *A Patch in Time.* Mill Valley, Calif.: Mill Valley Quilt Authority, 1973.

Hague, Harlan, and David J. Langum. *Thomas O. Larkin: A Life of Patriotism and Profit in Old California.* Norman and London: University of Oklahoma Press, 1990.

Hall, Carrie A., and Rose G. Kretsinger. *The Romance of the Patchwork Quilt in America.* Caldwell, Idaho: Caxton Printers, Ltd., 1935.

Hammond, George P., ed. *The Larkin Papers: Personal, Business and Official Correspondence of Thomas Oliver Larkin, Merchant and United States Consul in California.* Vol. 3. Berkeley and Los Angeles: University of California Press, 1952.

Harding, Deborah. *Red & White: American Redwork Quilts.* New York: Rizzoli, 2000.

Hartley, Florence. *The Ladies Hand Book of Fancy and Ornamental Work.* Philadelphia: J. W. Bradley, 1861.

Harper's Bazar. March 21, 1868 and July 25, 1885.

Heimann, Robert K. *Tobacco and Americans.* New York: McGraw-Hill, 1960.

History of Alameda County, California. Oakland, Calif.: M. W. Wood, 1883.

Holliday, J. S. *Rush for Riches: Gold Fever and the Making of California.* Berkeley, Los Angeles and London: Oakland Museum of California and University of California, 1999.

Holmes, Elmer Wallace. *History of Riverside, California.* Los Angeles: History Record Company, 1912.

Holmes, Kenneth L., ed. *Covered Wagon Women: Diaries & Letters from the Western Trails 1840–1890.* Vols. 1–11. Glendale, Calif. and Spokane, Wash.: The Arthur H. Clark Company, 1983–93.

Hussey, John Adam. "New Light upon Talbot H. Green." *California Historical Society Quarterly* 3 (1924): 32–63.

Jones, Roger W. *California from the Conquistadores to the Legends of Laguna.* Laguna Beach, Calif.: Rockledge Enterprises, 1997.

Joseph, Alvin M. Jr. *The Civil War in the American West.* New York: Alfred A. Knopf, 1992.

Kiracofe, Roderick. *The American Quilt.* New York: Clarkson Potter, 1993.

Larcom, Lucy. *A New England Childhood Outlined from Memory.* Boston and New York: Houghton, Mifflin and Company, 1892.

Laury, Jean Ray, and the California Heritage Quilt Project. *Ho for California! Pioneer Women and Their Quilts.* New York: E. P. Dutton, 1990.

Levy, Jo Ann. *They Saw the Elephant: Women in the California Gold Rush.* Norman: University of Oklahoma Press, 1992.

Lewis, Donovan. *Pioneers of California: True Stories of Early Settlers in the Golden State.* San Francisco: Scottwall Associates, 1993.

Maksel, Rebecca. "Migrant Madonna." *Smithsonian* (March 2000): 21–22.

Manns, William, and Elizabeth Clair Flood. *Cowboys & The Trappings of the Old West.* Santa Fe, N. Mex.: Zon International Publishing Company, 1997.

Marcy, Captain Randolph B. *The Prairie Traveler: A Hand-book for Overland Expeditions.* Washington, D.C.: War Department, 1859.

Masonic Symbols in American Decorative Arts. Exhibition Catalogue. Lexington, Mass.: Scottish Rite Masonic Museum of Our National Heritage, 1976.

McKinstry, George Jr. to Edward M. Kern. San Diego, Calif. September 23, 1851. MS 122. Fort Sutter Papers, Huntington Library, San Marino, Calif.

McLachlan, Diana. *A Common Thread: Quilts in the Yakima Valley.* Yakima, Wash.: Yakima Valley Museum & Historical Association, 1985.

Meadows, Don. "Early Laguna Beach." In *The Historical Volume and Reference Works,* vol. 3. Whittier, Calif.: Historical Publishers, 1963.

"Methodist News." *California Independent.* February 5, 1898.

Mitchell, Daniel J. B. "The Lessons of Ham and Eggs: California's 1938 and 1939 Pension Ballot Propositions." *Historical Society of Southern California, Southern California Quarterly* 82, no. 2 (Summer 2000): 193–218.

Montgomery, Florence M. *Printed Textiles: English and American Cottons and Linens 1700–1950.* New York: Viking Press, 1970.

———. *Textiles in America: 1650–1870.* New York: W. W. Norton, 1984.

Moore, Winston, and Marian Moore. *Out of the Frying Pan.* Los Angeles: DeVorss & Co., 1939.

Nowlin, William. *The Bark Covered House; or, Back in the Woods Again.* Chicago: The Lakeside Press, 1937.

Orange County Historical Society. *Orange County History Series* 2 (1932).

Ornamental Stitches for Embroidery. Lynn, Mass.: T. E. Parker, 1885.

Osborn, Arthur D. "A History of the Biggs, Butte County Area." Unpublished thesis paper, 1953.

Parker, Robert J. "The Wreck of the Star of the West." *The Quarterly: Historical Society of Southern California* 23, no. 1 (March 1941): 24–27.

Patterson, Tom. *A Colony for California.* Riverside, Calif.: The Museum Press, 1996.

Perry, Claire. *Pacifica Arcadia: Images of California 1600–1915.* New York and Oxford: Oxford University Press, 1999.

Peto, Florence. *American Quilts and Coverlets: A History of a Charming Native Art Together with a Manual of Instruction for Beginners.* New York: Chanticleer Press, 1949.

———. *Historic Quilts.* New York: American Historical Company, Inc., 1939.

Rae, Janet, Margaret Tucker, Dinah Travis, Pauline Adams, Bridget Long, Deryn O'Connor, and Tina Fenwick Smith. *Quilt Treasures of Great Britain.* Nashville, Tenn.: Rutledge Hill Press, 1996.

Rae, Janet. *The Quilts of the British Isles.* London: Constable, 1987.

RAWLINGS, LINDA, ed. *Dear General: The Private Letters of Annie E. Kennedy and John Bidwell 1866–1868.* Sacramento: California Department of Parks and Recreation, 1993.

REGNERY, DOROTHY. "Pioneering Women." *The Californian: Magazine of the California History Center Foundation* 8, no. 2: 6–9.

RHODES, LYNWOOD MARK. "Uncle Sam's 100th Birthday Party–1876." *The American Legion Magazine* (February 1973): 20–25ff.

RODECAPE, LOIS FOSTER. "Gilding the Sunflower: A Study of Oscar Wilde's Visit to San Francisco." *California Historical Society Quarterly* 19, no. 2 (June 1940): 97–112.

ROTHSTEIN, NATALIE, ed. *A Lady of Fashion: Barbara Johnson's Album of Styles and Fabrics.* London: Thames and Hudson, 1987.

SAVAGE, THOMAS C. *Los Tiempos Pasados de la Alta California: Requerdos de la Sra. Da. Juana Machado de Ridington.* 1878. MS in the Bancroft Library, University of California, Berkeley.

SIMMONS, MICHAEL. "Bringing Astronomy to an Isolated Mountaintop." *Reflections* (1983).

———. "Building the 60-inch Telescope." *Reflections* (1984).

———. "Entering a New Era in Solar Research." *Reflections* (1983).

SMYTHE, WILLIAM E. *History of San Diego.* Vol. 1. San Diego, Calif.: The History Company, 1908.

Sotheby's Catalogue. October 13, 2000.

STARR, KEVIN, AND RICHARD. J. ORSI, eds. *Rooted in Barbarous Soil: People, Culture, and Community in Gold Rush California.* Berkeley: University of California Press for the California Historical Society, 2000.

STEWART, GEORGE R. *The California Trail.* New York: McGraw-Hill, 1962.

The Stock Manual. Fort Worth, Tex.: George B. Loving, 1881.

SUTTER, JOHN TO P. B. READING. New Helvetia, Calif. October 7, 1845. MS in the California State Library, Sacramento, Calif.

———. January 29, 1846. MS in the California State Library, Sacramento, Calif.

SUTTER, JOHN ET AL. *New Helvetia Diary: A Record of Events Kept by John A. Sutter and His Clerks at New Helvetia, California, from September 9, 1845 to May 25 1848.* San Francisco: The Grabhorn Press in arrangement with The Society of California Pioneers, 1939.

VAN NOSTRAND, JEAN. *A Pictorial and Narrative History of Monterey Adobe Capital of California 1770–1847.* San Francisco: California Historical Society, 1968.

VALENTINE, MRS., ed. *The Girl's Companion: A Book of Pastimes in Work and Play.* London and New York: Frederick Warne and Co., n.d.

VINCENT, MARGARET. *The Ladies' Work Table: Domestic Needlework in Nineteenth-Century America.* Allentown, Pa.: Allentown Art Museum, 1988.

WALDVOGEL, MERIKAY. *Soft Covers for Hard Times: Quiltmaking & the Great Depression.* Nashville, Tenn.: Rutledge Hill Press, 1990.

WEIR, DULCIE. "The Career of a Crazy Quilt." *Godey's Lady's Book* 109 (July 1884): 77–82.

WILDE, OSCAR. *Philadelphia Press.* January 17, 1882.

YOUNG, JOHN R. "Reminiscences of John R. Young." *Utah Historical Quarterly* 3 (1930): 83–90.

Index

Page numbers in italics refer to illustrations; those followed by "n" refer to notes.

Edited by Shelly Kale

Designed by Sandy Bell

Proofed and indexed by Anita Keys

Photography supervised by Steve Oliver

Text type set in Truesdell

Display type set in Black Adder and Cantoria

Printed by Arti Grafiche Amilcare Pizzi SpA, Milan, Italy